Managing Your Money in Retirement

Managing Your Money in Retirement

Enjoy retirement to the full with this practical money guide

JOHN WHITELEY

How To Books

Published by How To Books Ltd,
3 Newtec Place, Magdalen Road,
Oxford OX4 1RE, United Kingdom.
Tel: (01865) 793806. Fax: (01865) 248780.
email: info@howtobooks.co.uk
www.howtobooks.co.uk

British Library Cataloguing in Publication Data
A catalogue record for this book is available from
the British Library.

Cover design Shireen Nathoo Design
Cover image Photodisc

Produced for How To Books by Deer Park Productions
Edited by Diana Brueton
Typeset by PDQ Typesetting, Newcastle-under-Lyme
Printed and bound by Cromwell Press, Trowbridge, Wiltshire

NOTE: The material contained in this book is set out in good
faith for general guidance and no liability can be accepted
for loss or expense incurred as a result of relying in particular
circumstances on statements made in the book. Laws and
regulations are complex and liable to change, and readers should
check the current position with the relevant authorities before
making personal arrangements.

Contents

List of Illustrations

Preface

You are approaching retirement, perhaps with trepidation, perhaps with anticipation. It may be something you have looked forward to, or it may be something you have dreaded. Whatever your attitude to retirement, make sure that your retirement is not spoiled by money problems.

Some people are overawed by finance, thinking that there is some mystique about it. Don't be put off by jargon. This book is for ordinary people like you who want to be in control of their own financial destiny. In this book, I try to explain simply the basic principles. You can then apply them to your own situation.

Your retirement should be the happiest time of your life. You can make your own decisions and plans, enjoy your family, do things you have always wanted to do, or take up new interests. I hope this book will be of help in a small way to enable you to get the most out of your retirement.

John Whiteley

1

Planning for Your Retirement

Your retirement is the longest holiday you will ever take. Make sure that you provide adequately to enjoy that holiday. The basic state pension is not really enough for most people's expectations. You may, of course, try to save for your retirement in any way you like. Simply putting money away in a savings account could be one way of tackling it, although it is unlikely to do the trick.

The tax incentives to provide for retirement are among the most generous there are. You have every encouragement to save for your retirement, in ways that are government approved and attract tax relief.

SERPS

If you are employed, you will be paying National Insurance Contributions. This is made up of a basic contribution and an additional earnings related contribution. The earnings related contribution goes towards providing you with an additional earnings related pension (State Earnings Related Pension Scheme or SERPS), when you retire.

Contracting out
You may opt to **contract out** of the SERPS scheme. In that case, any additional contributions that would have gone to the SERPS scheme must be diverted to a private pension scheme. This will be operated by your employer if there is a **superannuation** scheme. Otherwise, you will have to arrange your own scheme.

SUPERANNUATION SCHEMES

These are schemes run by employers to provide a pension when you retire. This need not necessarily be at the age of 65. Many employers provide for retirement much earlier. These schemes may be contributory or non-contributory (i.e. by the employer). Under a **contributory scheme** the employer's contribution may be related to the contribution you make (e.g. the employer may match any contribution you make up to a certain percentage of your salary), or it may be unrelated to your contribution.

Provided that the superannuation scheme meets the requirements of the Inland Revenue, contributions are tax deductible.

Benefits

Under an employer's superannuation scheme, the benefits at retirement may be a **final salary** scheme, or a **money purchase** scheme. A final salary scheme is one in which the pension is set at a proportion of your final salary at the date you retire, geared to the number of years' contributions you have made. Thus it may be expressed as, say, one sixtieth of a third of your final salary for every complete year you have contributed to the scheme.

A money purchase scheme operates in a different way. The contributions you make are credited to a fund, and at your retirement the fund is used to purchase an **annuity.**

Lump sums

Both types of scheme usually provide for part of the fund or pension to be commuted in return for a tax-free lump sum.

Death in service benefits

Both types of scheme also provide for a benefit to your dependants if you die before retiring. This is also based on either the salary at date of death, or the amount accumulated in the fund.

AVCs

This stands for Additional Voluntary Contributions. As the name implies, this means that you may make additional contributions to the superannuation scheme. The total contributions may not exceed 15% of your salary.

STAKEHOLDER PENSIONS

At the time of writing, Stakeholder Pensions are in the planning stage – they will be introduced early in 2001. They are aimed mainly at those earning in the range of £10,000 – £20,000 per year. They will have to be offered by employers, and they will incur only minimal charges. There will also be the opportunity for self-employed or even non-employed people to take out Stakeholder Pensions and still benefit from full tax relief.

PERSONAL PENSION SCHEMES

These are plans, approved by the Inland Revenue and run by insurance and pension companies, which are long-term savings schemes, designed to provide for retirement. Because of the generous tax advantages, they have rules that must be adhered to in order to qualify for the tax concessions.

Qualifying earnings

First you must have qualifying earnings to be able to put your money into one of these schemes. This means that your earnings must come from:

- self-employment, or

- employment with an employer that does not have a pension scheme of its own, or

- furnished holiday letting income.

If you do not have earnings which qualify, the Inland Revenue can instruct the pension company to repay to you any contributions you have paid.

Benefits

The other main condition is that the benefits may only be paid to between the ages of 50 and 75. There are, however, several categories of occupation which allow earlier retirement for the purposes of drawing benefits. These include many sports activities, such as wrestlers, downhill skiers, footballers, jockeys, etc. There are also some other types of occupation such as models and dancers, included in the list.

The pension you receive is an annuity purchased by your fund. An annuity is a regular sum, paid monthly, quarterly, or annually, for the rest of your life. The rates are worked out by actuaries.

Annuities can be of fixed amounts, or escalating amounts. The increases can be of a fixed amount each year (generally 3% or 5%), or linked to the retail prices index. The annuities can also be for the sole life of the beneficiary, or for the joint lives of the beneficiary and his or her spouse. A minimum guarantee period of, say, five or ten years can be provided if requested. This means that if the beneficiary dies within that period, the survivors get the income for the rest of that guarantee period. There are also 'impaired life' annuities. This means that if the beneficiary is suffering from a life threatening illness, then because the life span is not so long, the annuity rate is increased.

Death benefit

If you die before taking the retirement benefits, then the pension policy will state what benefit your dependants will receive. In some older retirement annuity policies, the death benefit was only a return of contributions, with or without a nominal rate of interest. Currently the best practice is for the value of the accumulated fund to be paid as the death benefit. This is certainly one of the key points to look for in a policy.

Tax-free lump sum

When you take your pension, you need not take all of it in the form of a regular pension. Part of the fund may be taken as a tax-free lump sum. At present the regulations allow you to take up to 25% of the fund as a lump sum. It is nearly always beneficial to take this lump sum. This allows you to invest the lump sum, enjoy the income, and still have the capital available if you need it, or to pass on to your survivors. Clearly this is better; otherwise the whole fund is tied up in the annuity and there is no access to the capital.

Open market option

When the policy matures, and you want to take your pension, you have the right to take the fund from your pension company and shop around for the best value pension. This is because the pension offered by each company is determined by its own annuity rates. These rates vary, and shopping around enables you to find the best value. This 'open market option' must be written into the pension contract to enable it to qualify for the tax advantages.

CHOOSING A POLICY

If you are considering taking out a policy, there are a bewildering number of choices available, and an equally bewildering number of salesmen trying to sell them to you. Bear in mind that they are earning their living, in the form of commission on these policies. The adviser you use may be independent or an employee of the company, but they still have a living to earn. Some companies advertise the fact that they do not pay commission to intermediaries. However, they still have their own sales force to pay.

However, the fact that a salesman gets commission does not necessarily mean that what they are trying to sell you is not good value. The following are some points to look for when choosing a pension:

What is the basis of the fund growth?
The funds are usually **unit linked** or **with profit**.

Unit linked
This means that the premiums buy you a certain number of units in a fund or funds provided by the pension company. Like **unit trusts** (see Chapter 3), there are various types of funds. The prices are quoted in the financial press, and the value of your pension fund at any time is the value of the units, multiplied by the number of units you hold. This means, of course, that the value can fall as well as rise.

With profit funds
With these the investment profits each year are credited to your account, as a 'bonus declaration'. The bonuses are added to the value of your fund each year, and there is also usually a 'terminal bonus' added when the policy matures. The annual bonuses cannot be taken away once they have been added to your fund. Although it may seem preferable to have profits added in this way, the 'with profit' policies usually keep a reserve back in good years to even out the growth.

What is the charging structure?
Many companies pay commission, and, particularly in the case of 'regular premium' policies, this means there is a large deduction from your fund in the first year or two. Thus it could take your fund a long time to recuperate from this reduction. This is known as 'front end loading'.

How flexible is the policy?
Do you want to pay regular premiums, or a single premium? Does your policy give you the opportunity to suspend premiums if necessary? If you are paying regular monthly or yearly premiums,

can you add on single premiums at a later date?

What is the basis of the benefit if you die before taking the pension?
You should always look for the fund value as the benefit, rather than return of premiums, even with interest.

Retirement annuity policies
These were the precursor to the personal pension schemes. They were available to self-employed people. Although these are no longer available to start as new policies, many people who started them still have them in force. They were similar in many ways to the personal pension policies, but the rules differed in some respects. One of the main differences is that the age at which benefits may be taken is between 60 and 75. Also, the tax-free lump sum is calculated differently from the personal pension policies, and is usually rather more.

INCOME DRAWDOWNS

Since 1995 it has been possible to opt for an **income drawdown** instead of taking the full benefits at retirement age. The theory is that annuity rates may not be particularly advantageous when you start drawing your pension. This has meant in the past that you could have been 'locked in' to a mediocre annuity rate for the rest of your life. The opportunity is now there for you to defer taking the full benefits from your pension fund, but instead to 'draw down' a certain amount every year from the fund – within certain limits, of course. The fund continues, but is depleted by the drawdowns each year, until such time as the benefits are taken – this must be by the age of 75.

Currently, insurance companies are offering higher than usual commission to intermediaries for drawdown schemes than for the normal annuities. This has led to the fear that drawdowns could be recommended even when they may not be the best value.

PHASED RETIREMENT

If the amount in your pension fund is adequate, you could opt for phased retirement. This is particularly useful for a person who wishes to retire from work gradually. If you have been able to make contributions to several different funds, you could start taking benefits from one of the funds, while reducing the amount you work, and gradually take benefits from the other funds year by year, until you reach full retirement.

If you have not been able to contribute to several funds, some companies will allow you to convert your pension fund into a number of smaller funds, and to phase the benefits from them. As with income drawdown, however, this sort of scheme will normally only be viable for funds in excess of about £100,000.

CHECKLIST

- Approved pension plans and superannuation schemes are amongst the best long-term savings opportunities. They give tax relief at your highest rate, and provide attractive alternatives when taking the benefits. However, they are long-term, and the capital is locked up absolutely until the benefits can be taken. You have no access to the capital.

- There are superannuation schemes, if you are employed. These may be contributory or non-contributory. They may be based on money purchase benefits, or final salary benefits. There is also the government SERPS, out of which you may contract.

- Personal pension policies are available if you are in non-pensionable employment, or in self-employment. The retirement annuity policies are no longer available but many are still in force. Policies may be with profit or unit linked. They may also be linked with mortgages.

- Drawdown schemes are available – but usually only for funds in excess of £100,000. Phased retirement can also be planned into the benefits.

CASE STUDIES

Alison

Alison's new job qualifies her for joining the firm's superannuation scheme, under which the company matches her contributions. She decides on a modest amount to start saving, confident that she can take it with her if she should change jobs in the future.

Brian

Brian has been saving with his company's superannuation scheme for some years. He now feels that he can put more of his savings in, and in fact this is a main concern of his. He looks around, and asks his company about the opportunities for putting more into their scheme. He decides to put as much as he can into the company scheme, and if there is any left over to put it into additional voluntary contributions.

Colin

Colin was employed until he was 40, and is now self-employed. He had a company pension scheme which was frozen when he left his employment. He has been contributing to various personal pension schemes since he became self-employed, and now, approaching 60, he wants to retire. He realises that he will have to bridge the gap until he reaches 65 and can draw the state pension. He consults his independent financial adviser.

The total value in all his pension funds is now nearly £300,000. After taking advice he decides to take out some of his pensions, by taking the open market option, and also taking the maximum tax-free lump sum. He decides to reduce gradually his business involvement over the next five years, and to phase in gradually taking the benefits from his pension schemes. He will be fully retired by the age of 65.

PERSONAL EVALUATION

1. Do you feel that you can put off providing for your retirement until later? If so, have you done the sums?

2. Have you considered all the options open to you?

3. Do you feel that you need to take advice about your pensions?

2

Principles of Investing

WHAT DO YOU WANT TO DO?

If you aim for nothing, you will probably hit it. Many people feel they would like to save or invest, but it remains a vague feeling. They may succeed in putting aside some money in a savings account of some sort, but it goes no further. They have no purpose or aim in their saving. The savings they have may be a nice little nest egg, but if it has no direct purpose it can too easily get used up on the first emergency, or even the first whim, that comes along.

Make it your first task to sit down and think about your aims. This will help you to structure your savings and investments. For example, if you want to save for your retirement, you will want to put your savings in a home where you cannot touch them until your retirement date. Otherwise you might be tempted to use the money for something else, and find yourself short when you come to retire.

Here are some of the most common aims for saving:

- generating an income
- protecting your capital
- fighting inflation
- providing for your retirement
- passing on your wealth to the next generation
- putting a deposit on a house
- paying for education of your children or grandchildren
- having the holiday of a lifetime
- buying an expensive item such as a boat
- replacing a car.

Changing your objectives

You may well have a different set of objectives at different points of your life. As a young person you may have wanted that flashy sports car, or the latest in windsurfing gear. Later you settle into married life, and buy a house or trade up to a better one. Children come along and you think about their education. In middle life you are more and more concerned about approaching retirement, and how to provide for that. As last you retire, and now you want to supplement your income from your savings. Some years into retirement you may think about passing on your wealth to your successors.

At all times be aware of your changing circumstances, and plan your savings with them in mind. Changes usually happen slowly, and we do not always recognise them. Therefore take time every so often – say every five years – to review where your life is and where it is going. Then make any changes necessary to your saving habits.

GENERATING AN INCOME

If you tried to live on the basic state pension, you might well find it difficult. Many people use their accumulated savings to generate an income to supplement their basic pension. If this is your aim, then invest your savings in a form which will generate this income for you.

It is always wise to bear in mind the effect of inflation, so try to obtain from your savings an income that has at least the possibility of escalating year by year, particularly if you have no other income.

PROTECTING YOUR CAPITAL AGAINST INFLATION

Protecting your capital and fighting inflation are really the same objective. If inflation is high, the real value of your savings gets eroded. For example, if inflation is at 10% per year, your money will buy 10% less next year than it bought this year. This only has to continue for five years for your money to be halved in value.

This is bad enough when applied to income, but even worse when you consider the effect on your savings. This effect is particularly relevant in planning for retirement. You are wise to start saving for retirement as early as possible. Therefore you could start saving when your retirement is 30 or even 40 years away. Even with fairly low rates of inflation – less than 5% – your savings would be severely eroded in 30 or 40 years' time. Therefore your main objective would be to save in a form that protects your savings against inflation.

Having your cake and eating it

You may decide that you would like the best of both worlds. You would like an income from your savings but you would also like to protect the capital. You can use certain types of investment that purport to do that. However, they inevitably represent a compromise of some kind.

A 'pure growth' type of investment will not provide much of an income, if any. A 'pure income' type of investment will not usually be very outstanding for its capital growth. An investment which tries to provide both aspects is usually a split investment of some kind: half the investment is put into a growth-type investment and the other half in an income-type investment. The income is halved and the growth potential is halved.

This leads us to the first two of my **Golden Rules of Investing**:

---

1. You cannot buck the market, so do not try to.
2. If something seems too good to be true, it probably is.

These two rules are really different ways of saying the same thing. In saying that you cannot buck the market, you recognise that the law of supply and demand has created certain rates of return on different types of savings and investments. There will always be variations within a certain range. For example, shares in companies in the same sector (say, insurance companies) will offer a similar return.

However, if any one investment in a certain field offers a rate of return which is significantly out of step with others in the same field, there is usually a significant risk element attached.

USING YOUR CRYSTAL BALL

Unless you are endowed with powers of second sight, you do not know what the future holds. One in three marriages ends in divorce, and a divorce can seriously upset the best planned savings and investment strategy. Divorce may be the most obvious wild card in the pack, but there are many other things which can cause your plans to go awry – redundancy, ill health, etc.

It is always a good idea to try to make your savings as flexible as possible. Ask questions about any investment you undertake, such as:

- Can I unscramble it if necessary?
- Is it readily encashable?
- Is the value liable to fall as well as rise?
- Can I pass it on easily to my descendants?

PLANNING BEYOND THE GRAVE

One consideration which may loom large in your thinking is how to pass your savings on to the next generation. Or perhaps you may have a favourite charity which you would like to benefit after your death.

If these are your concerns, then you must consider another dimension to planning your savings. That is, of course, minimising **Inheritance Tax**. This is dealt with in Chapter 10.

Ordering your priorities

As valid as these concerns may be, they should be kept in perspective. Do not jeopardise your present plans for the sake of passing on the most you can. Make sure that you are adequately provided for in the here and now.

EVALUATING THE RISK/REWARD RELATIONSHIP

Here is the third **Golden Rule of Investing**.

3. There is no reward without risk.

When making your plans for savings and investments, you must decide about the degree of risk with which you are happy. This does not mean that your degree of risk is set in concrete. You may change your attitude to risk at different times of your life, or depending on how much money you have to invest. Remember one of the first principles – review your circumstances regularly (and this includes a changing attitude to risk) and be ready to change your savings plan if necessary.

Beware of 'guaranteed'

Many investments are marketed on advertising which promotes the safety aspect. They are targeted at what are known as 'risk averse investors'. You may see the word 'guaranteed' feature in advertise-ments or in the name of the product. Beware of this word! Find out all you can about the investment before committing your money. In particular, read the small print to find out exactly what is guaranteed.

EVALUATING RISK

There are some obvious pointers to a high-risk investment.

Assessing the quality of information

If you get chatting to a fellow at the pub, who you only know by sight, and he recommends a sure-fire tip for the 2.30 at Newmarket, you would not put all your savings on it. If that same fellow offered to sell you some shares in a gold-prospecting company which had just found gold in the wilds of Alaska, your reaction would probably be the same.

Your assessment of the risk is coloured by your judgement of the quality of the information. One of the main factors in this is the trust and confidence you have in the person giving you the information.

Here is the fourth **Golden Rule of Investing**.

> 4. You cannot have too much information.

But information always comes from someone. It may be the man in the pub, or the pages of the *Financial Times*, or anywhere in between those two extremes.

If you are at all uncertain, try to corroborate the information with someone in whom you have confidence.

What is behind it?

All forms of saving and investment have something behind them. Take, for instance, a building society account. By saving in this you are putting money into a large pool which is then loaned to people buying a house. That is very simple to understand, and very 'transparent'. You can easily see that the ultimate investment of the money is in bricks and mortar.

Other forms of investment may not be quite so transparent. A name such as General Amalgamated Consolidated Portfolio PLC would not really give any clue as to what your money would be invested in. So always make a point of trying to find out what is behind it. Is it a chain of seedy nightclubs? It is an international group exploiting the resources of the third world?

● Remember – you cannot have too much information.

You may be considering investing in a **unit trust** or **investment trust**. As we shall see in Chapter 3, these work on the principle of spreading the risk. They use money from many small investors into a large fund, which is then spread in a wide variety of companies. But you then need to look further into it. Most unit trusts or investment trusts specialise in certain types of company or investment, or certain geographical areas. For instance, a trust labelled as 'high income' or 'high yield' will probably have all, or a large part, of its investments in fixed interest **government stocks**, or other fixed interest investments. A 'growth' trust will probably be invested to a large extent in smaller companies judged to have potential for growth.

How big is it?
A further indicator of risk is the size of the company or fund into which you are investing. Take the example of the unit trust again, look at the literature. What is the size of the fund? Is it several millions. Or is it tens of millions? Or for a company, what is the total market value of all the shares in issue? (This is known as the market capitalisation.)

When you know how big the fund or company is, you can make your own decisions. This is one area where big may be beautiful, but smaller companies or funds often provide better performance.

How marketable is it?
Another factor in judging the degree of risk attached to a particular investment is the extent of marketability. The ultimate in marketability for company shares is, of course, the **Stock Exchange**. In order to qualify to be traded on the Stock Exchange, a company must meet stringent requirements. Anybody owning shares in those companies may sell them openly to any other willing buyer. The number of transactions on the Stock Exchange runs into millions every week.

At the other end on the scale could be a small family company. The shares may be owned by, say, mother, father and two sons. If one of them wanted to sell their shares, the rules of the company may well say that they may only sell them to directors of the company. Even if this rule did not exist, it would not be easy to find a buyer outside the family willing to buy shares in that company.

- In general terms, shares in smaller companies are not as marketable as shares in bigger companies.

Short-term or long-term?

In judging the degree of risk, you need to think about whether your investment is going to be short-term or long-term. This will affect your attitude to risk.

If you want to invest long-term you must take the effects of inflation into account. This is obviously not as important for the short-term. Thus if you want to put some money away for a specific purpose, and you know that you will be drawing it out in say one year or less, then a deposit with a bank or building society represents a low-risk investment. For the same length of time, investing in shares on the stock market would be a high risk, because you would not be sure that you would not make a loss, especially when dealing costs are taken into account.

If you want to invest long-term, and not have to dip into the capital, then a deposit in a bank or building society would be a high risk. It would be virtually certain that the capital invested would be worth less in, say, ten or 15 years than it is now. That is because inflation will have eroded the purchasing power of the money.

Investing in shares for the long-term is not as great a risk as for the short-term. Historically, prices of shares have at least kept up with inflation. If you seriously believed that inflation would be negative – i.e. deflation – then the above advice would be reversed.

Timing

Timing has an effect on your judgement of risk. This is particularly so when looking at investments with a fixed term. The fact of a fixed term means that the circumstances at the time the investment matures are fixed. It may be that the value you receive at maturity is dependent on circumstances such as the amount of the **Stock Exchange Index**. Or the circumstances at the time of maturity may not be favourable for re-investing the proceeds.

- As a general rule, investments with a fixed term are more risky than ones which are not fixed.

Taking a risk

When you have made your assessment of the risk involved, you can then apply your own principles of how much risk to take when making your investments. If you are happy to take a fairly high risk, at least with some of your money, then you will want to look at the best returns available.

Playing safe

If you decide that some or all of your money should be in low-risk investments and savings, then you will look very carefully at the degree of safety. If there are any 'guarantees', you will want to find out exactly what is guaranteed. Then, within these guidelines, find the best return you can get for your money.

CHECKLIST

- Sort out your aims and objectives.
- Review your objectives regularly.
- Decide whether you want income, capital protection, or both.
- Try to keep your options open.
- Think about the next generation.
- Decide your approach to risk.
- Evaluate the risk factor in any investment.

CASE STUDIES

Brenda

Brenda is still about five years off retirement age, but has just been widowed. She has not worked for many years. Her husband had a good job, and they lived well on his salary. His life was insured, so she has a capital sum. She wants to be able to live as well as she can from investing that capital. She might decide to take some work, but she is not sure yet. She would like to be able to take a little time over this decision. She would like to be able to make the decision to take some work not because it is forced on her by financial pressures, but to help her adjust to life on her own.

Brenda is therefore looking to maximise her income. However, she is still relatively young and has many years ahead of her. She wants to protect the capital as much as possible, without upsetting the primary aim of generating income.

Charles

Charles is married and has just retired. He has a company pension, and a life assurance endowment policy is due to mature. His wife is a few years younger than him, and she wants to continue working for the time being. Charles does not yet have any positive ideas about what to do with his endowment. He has not yet budgeted for living in retirement, and has a vague idea that with his company pension and the state pension he will manage, although he realises that he will not be as well off as before. He always had it in mind that he and his wife would take a cruise when he retired.

A friend takes him aside and tells him he must plan his lifestyle in retirement, and plan his finances as well. He starts to take this seriously, and when the endowment matures decides to put it for the time being into a building society account which gives him good interest, but where he can realise the money without any undue delay.

PERSONAL EVALUATION

1. Do you know what you expect to achieve from your savings? How can you make a working plan to help you achieve your goals?

2. Do you have an idea of where you are going in your life? How can the savings plan be tailored to fit your plans?

3. How can you plan to cope with uncertainties and unexpected calamities?

3

Investing in Stocks and Shares

DEALING IN STOCKS AND SHARES

The stock exchanges of the world were set up to provide a market place for those wishing to buy or sell shares. The growth of limited liability companies produced a need for shareholders to be able to buy or sell shares. Without this facility, far fewer people would have been willing to invest in companies. For the purposes of this book, we are looking at the way the London Stock Exchange works.

To trade in shares, you must deal through a **stockbroker**. The stockbroker deals on the Stock Exchange through **market makers**, or through the **SETS** trading system on the London Stock Exchange.

Market makers
Market makers are traders who deal only with brokers. If a broker approaches a market maker stating that he wants to deal in a certain quantity of a particular share, the market maker will quote two prices – one at which he will offer to buy, the other at which he will offer to sell. The difference between the buying price and the selling price is called the spread. If the broker is satisfied, he will then tell the market maker whether he wants to buy or sell, and the quantity.

SETS
This is a computer system which displays offers for sale and offers for purchase with the quantities on offer for shares. The computer then matches up the buyers and sellers. At the time of writing, this system deals with most of the shares on the 'top 250' index. As recent experience has shown, any failure in the computer system can sabotage the whole market!

Settling the bills
When a deal has been made, the stockbroker will send you an account. This shows the number of shares dealt, the price of dealing, and any expenses such as stamp duty and their own commission. See Figure 1.

Laing & Cruickshank Investment Management Ltd

Member of The London Stock Exchange
Regulated by The Securities & Futures Authority
Member of The Credit Lyonnais Group

BROADWALK HOUSE 5 APPOLD STREET LONDON EC2A 2DA
TELEPHONE 0171-588 2800 TELEX 9419248 LACIM FAX 0171-374 0066 DX 699 LONDON/CITY

Contract Note/Advice Note

SUBJECT TO THE RULES AND REGULATIONS OF THE LONDON STOCK EXCHANGE

WE HAVE AS AGENTS SOLD BY ORDER AND FOR THE ACCOUNT OF

ON 23 FEB 98 (TAX POINT) AT 4.01PM

***** FOR SETTLEMENT ON 02 MAR 98 *****

866 BRITISH TELECOMMUNICATIONS
ORD 25P

	@ £ 5.995				£	5,191.67
				LESS		
£5,191.67 @	1.85%	=	96.05	CONTRACT FEE	£	25.00
				COMMISSION	£	96.05
				VAT		
				EXEMPT	£	0.00
				TOTAL CREDIT	£	5,070.62

TO ENSURE PROMPT SETTLEMENT PLEASE SEND US THE RELEVANT DOCUMENTS. WE
RESERVE THE RIGHT TO RECOUP ANY COSTS INCURRED THROUGH LATE DELIVERY.
****

BARGAIN NO. QBO0499B00
52026C /76 (0-140-843)

DUPLICATE COPY

E&OE

Registered in England No1325665
Registered Office: - as above
VAT No 447 2599 17

Fig. 1. Stockbroker's contract note.

Laing & Cruickshank Investment Management Ltd

Registered in England No 1325665
Registered Office Broadwalk House.
5 Appold St, London EC2A 2DA

VAT Regn No 447 2599 17

Member of The London Stock Exchange
Regulated by The Securities & Futures Authority
Member of The Credit Lyonnais Group

Broadwalk House
5, Appold Street
London EC2A 2DA

Telephone 0171-588 2800
Facsimile 0171-374 0066
DX 699 London/City

Statement of Account
Period To   13/03/98

Ref.

Page   1

RE ACCOUNT :

Date	Transaction	Debit	Credit
	Pounds Sterling Brought Forward Balance	£ 0.00	
	Current Statement Period Transactions		
17/02/98	BGHT 800 BRITISH PETROLEUM CO ORD 25P QBH0273B00 @ £ 7.935 EX-DIV Value date 03/03/98	£ 6,522.18	
17/02/98	BGHT 6300 AMEC 6.5P (NET) CUM CNV PRF 50P QBH0279B00 @ £ 0.98 Value date 03/03/98	£ 6,344.09	
17/02/98	SOLD 2600 FLEMING AMERICAN INVESTMENT TRUST 7% CNV UNS LN STK 1999 QBH0284B00 @ £ 505 Value date 03/03/98		£ 12,904.10
	Balance as at 13/03/98		£ 37.83

E&OE

Fig. 2. Stockbroker's settlement account.

Settlement is five working days afterwards. If you have bought, the amount is payable to your stockbroker. If you have sold, the stockbroker will pay you. You may, of course, have sold one shareholding and bought another. In this case, all transactions on the same day will be aggregated and the net amount will be due from you or to you. See Figure 2.

CHOOSING AND USING A STOCKBROKER

Finding a stockbroker who will take you on as a client is not too difficult. They are in business, and will not turn away the right sort of client. The best introduction to a stockbroker is through a friend or relation who is already a client. They will be able to tell you how good they feel the service is. Alternatively, a professional adviser such as an accountant or solicitor can probably recommend a stockbroker to you.

Once you have a stockbroker, stay with him or her unless there is some serious problem. The relationship you build up over the years will prove very useful. The service you get from your stockbroker will be one of:

- advisory
- execution only
- discretionary.

Advisory
This means that the stockbroker advises you either when you request advice on, say, whether to sell, or investing a lump sum, or when he or she feels that a particular purchase or sale would be a good move.

Execution only
This means that the stockbroker will make a certain deal for you, simply on your instructions. They may have no opinion, or they may advise against it, but if you still give the order to go ahead, they carry out your request.

Discretionary
This means that you give the stockbroker the right to manage your shares. The stockbroker will hold your shares in a nominee company, in an account that is designated in your name. They will then go ahead and make any deals which they consider to be right for you.

HAVING YOUR PORTFOLIO MANAGED

A stockbroker will normally take on a **portfolio** of shares provided that it is of a reasonable size. At present, this would probably mean a minimum of £50,000. He or she would then load the details on the computer, and provide you with a valuation list. This would then be updated and sent to you periodically, typically once or twice a year. Figure 3 shows what a typical valuation statement looks like. It gives the following information:

- Summary of investments by sector. This shows the total value broken down into the different sectors of the economy.

- Geographical analysis. This shows how the investments are spread through the world.

- Individual details. This shows each investment separately, and gives the following details:
  - Holding. This means the number of shares of each type.

  - Market price. This is the price of the share at the date of the valuation.

  - Market value. This is the total value of the shares, obtained by multiplying the holding by the market price.

  - Book cost. This is the actual price at which you bought the investment. By comparing this with the market value, you can see whether you are currently showing a profit or a loss.

  - Dividend rate. This is the latest declared dividend rate of the company, and is expressed in money terms per share.

  - Estimated gross income. This is the dividend rate multiplied by the number of shares. It shows you how much you should receive in the current year from the investment.

  - Dividend yield. This is the income expressed as a percentage of the market value. It means that if you bought that investment at the market price on the day of the valuation, the actual income as a percentage of the price is different from the dividend rate. This is called the yield and is the only safe measure of comparing one investment with another.

  - Dividends due. This tells you when the forthcoming dividends are likely to be paid. There are usually two dividends

Laing & Cruickshank Investment Management Ltd

Member of The London Stock Exchange
Regulated by The Securities & Futures Authority
Member of the Credit Lyonnais Group

Portfolio Valuation

Date 22 Aug 1997

Ref.

Page   1

Security description	Holding	Market price	Market value	Book cost	Dividend rate	Estimated Gross income	%Div. yield	Dividends Due
FIXED INTEREST								
UNITED KINGDOM								
FIXED INTEREST/CONVERTIBLES								
BRITISH FUNDS								
EXCHEQUER 9 3/4% STK 1998	£ 7,051.23	£ 101 34 days	£ 7,122 £ 64	£ 6,433	9.75%	£ 687	9.65	Jan Jul
CONVERSION 9% STK 2000	£ 6,501.63	£ 104 3/16 172 days XD	£ 6,774 £ 276	£ 6,298	9.00%	£ 585	8.64	Mar Sep
TREASURY 8% STK 2003	£ 14,494.29	£ 104 1/8 73 days	£ 15,092 £ 232	£ 14,502	8.00%	£ 1,160	7.68	Jun Dec
TREASURY 8% LN 2002/06	£ 6,484.22	£ 102 17/32 139 days	£ 6,648 £ 198	£ 6,372	8.00%	£ 519	7.80	Apr Oct
TREASURY 8 1/2% LN 2007	£ 9,840.06	£ 109 5/16 37 days	£ 10,756 £ 85	£ 10,000	8.50%	£ 836	7.78	Jan Jul
FIXED INTEREST TOTAL			**£ 47,247**	**£ 43,606**		**£ 3,787**	**8.16**	
EQUITY								
UNITED KINGDOM								
MINERAL EXTRACTION								
EXTRACTIVE INDUSTRIES								
RIO TINTO ORD 10P(REGD)	680	999.5p	£ 6,797	£ 6,681	£ 0.32	£ 270	3.97	Oct Apr Apr

Fig. 3. Portfolio valuation.

35

Member of The London Stock Exchange
Regulated by The Securities & Futures Authority
Member of the Credit Lyonnais Group

Laing & Cruickshank Investment Management Ltd

Portfolio Valuation

Date 22 Aug 1997
Ref.
Page 4

Security description	Holding	Market price	Market value	Book cost	Dividend rate	Estimated Gross income	%Div. yield	Dividends Due
BANKS, RETAIL (CONT.)								
ROYAL BANK OF SCOTLAND GROUP ORD 25P	840	593p	£ 4,981	£ 4,136	£ 0.19 II	£ 204	4.09	Jul Feb
Sector Total			£ 9,944	£ 6,781		£ 326	3.28	
INSURANCE								
COMMERCIAL UNION ORD 25P	1,320	722.5p XD	£ 9,537	£ 3,085	£ 0.31 II	£ 513	5.38	Nov May
Class Total			£ 19,481	£ 9,866		£ 839	4.31	
INVESTMENT TRUSTS								
INVESTMENT TRUSTS								
ALLIANCE TRUST ORD STK 25P	1,040	£ 24.29	£ 25,262	£ 8,652	£ 0.57 II	£ 741	2.93	Oct Apr
SECURITIES TRUST OF SCOTLAND ORD 25P	17,200	114p	£ 19,608	£ 18,463	£ 0.04	£ 806	4.11	Dec Jul
Class Total			£ 44,870	£ 27,115		£ 1,547	3.45	
EQUITY TOTAL			£ 181,235	£ 89,596		£ 7,218	3.98	
GRAND TOTAL			£ 228,482	£ 133,201		£ 11,005	4.83	

Fig. 3. Cont/d.

Laing & Cruickshank Investment Management Ltd

Portfolio Summary

Member of The London Stock Exchange
Regulated by The Securities & Futures Authority
Member of the Crédit Lyonnais Group

Date 22 Aug 1997

Ref

Page 5

Description	Book cost	Market value	Estimated Gross income	% Book cost	% Market value	Gross income	Gross yield %
FIXED INTEREST							
FIXED INTEREST/CONVERTIBLES							
BRITISH FUNDS	£ 43,606	£ 47,247	£ 3,787	32.74	20.68	34.41	8.16
FIXED INTEREST TOTAL	£ 43,606	£ 47,247	£ 3,787	32.74	20.68	34.41	8.16
EQUITY							
MINERAL EXTRACTION							
EXTRACTIVE INDUSTRIES	£ 6,681	£ 6,797	£ 270	5.02	2.97	2.45	3.97
OIL, INTEGRATED	£ 7,000	£ 11,955	£ 332	5.25	5.23	3.02	2.78
MINERAL EXTRACTION TOTAL	£ 13,681	£ 18,752	£ 602	10.27	8.21	5.47	3.21
GENERAL MANUFACTURERS							
CHEMICALS	£ 6,519	£ 9,737	£ 386	4.89	4.26	3.51	3.97
DIVERSIFIED INDUSTRIALS	£ 6,865	£ 5,043	£ 353	5.15	2.21	3.20	6.99
ENGINEERING	£ 9,559	£ 20,338	£ 950	7.18	8.90	8.64	4.67
ENGINEERING, VEHICLES	£ 5,033	£ 14,214	£ 411	3.78	6.22	3.73	2.89
GENERAL MANUFACTURERS TOTAL	£ 27,976	£ 49,333	£ 2,100	21.00	21.59	19.09	4.26
CONSUMER GOODS							
FOOD MANUFACTURERS	£ 1,496	£ 9,384	£ 348	1.12	4.11	3.17	3.71
PHARMACEUTICALS	£ 1,138	£ 14,404	£ 333	0.85	6.30	3.03	2.31
TOBACCO	£ 1,044	£ 17,168	£ 1,232	0.78	7.51	11.19	7.17
CONSUMER GOODS TOTAL	£ 3,678	£ 40,956	£ 1,913	2.76	17.93	17.38	4.67
SERVICES							
TRANSPORT	£ 7,279	£ 7,844	£ 216	5.46	3.43	1.96	2.75
FINANCIALS							
BANKS, RETAIL	£ 6,781	£ 9,944	£ 326	5.09	4.35	2.96	3.28
INSURANCE	£ 3,085	£ 9,537	£ 513	2.32	4.17	4.66	5.38
FINANCIALS TOTAL	£ 9,866	£ 19,481	£ 839	7.41	8.53	7.63	4.31
INVESTMENT TRUSTS							
INVESTMENT TRUSTS	£ 27,115	£ 44,870	£ 1,547	20.36	19.64	14.06	3.45

Fig. 3. Cont/d.

Laing & Cruickshank Investment Management Ltd

Portfolio Summary

Member of The London Stock Exchange
Regulated by The Securities & Futures Authority
Member of the Credit Lyonnais Group

Description	Book cost	Market value	Estimated Gross income	% Book cost	% Market value	% Gross income	Gross yield %
INVESTMENT TRUSTS (CONT.)							
EQUITY TOTAL	£ 89,596	£ 181,235	£ 7,218	67.26	79.32	65.59	3.98
GRAND TOTAL	£ 133,201	£ 228,482	£ 11,005	100.00	100.00	100.00	4.83

Fig. 3. Cont/d.

Laing & Cruickshank Investment Management Ltd

Portfolio Summary

Member of The London Stock Exchange
Regulated by The Securities & Futures Authority
Member of the Credit Lyonnais Group

Date 22 Aug 1997
Ref.
Page 7

Description	Book cost	Market value	Estimated Gross income	% Book cost	% Market value	% Gross income	Gross yield %
GEOGRAPHICAL ANALYSIS							
FIXED INTEREST							
UNITED KINGDOM	£ 43,606	£ 47,247	£ 3,787	32.74	20.68	34.41	8.16
EQUITY							
UNITED KINGDOM	£ 89,596	£ 181,235	£ 7,218	67.26	79.32	65.59	3.98
GRAND TOTAL	£ 133,201	£ 228,482	£ 11,005	100.00	100.00	100.00	4.83

Fig. 3. Cont/d.

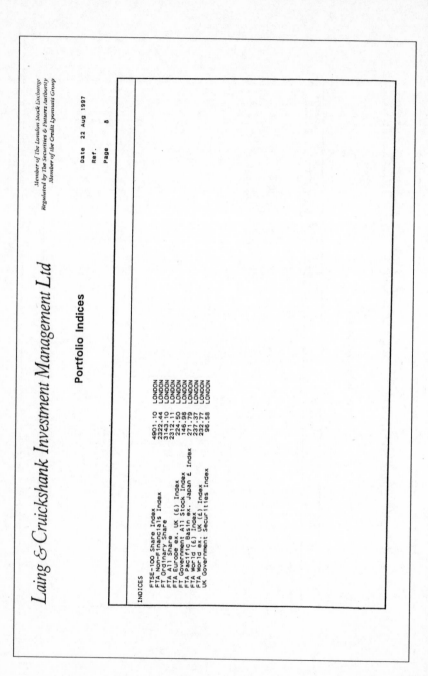

Laing & Cruickshank Investment Management Ltd

Member of The London Stock Exchange
Regulated by The Securities & Futures Authority
Member of the Credit Lyonnais Group

Portfolio Indices

Date   22 Aug 1997

Ref.

Page   8

INDICES

FTSE-100 Share Index	4901.10	LONDON
FTA Non-Financials Index	2322.44	LONDON
FT Ordinary Share	3143.10	LONDON
FTA All Share	2312.11	LONDON
FTA Europe ex. UK (£) Index	224.50	LONDON
FT Government All Stock Index	146.98	LONDON
FTA Pacific Basin ex. Japan E Index	271.79	LONDON
FTA World (£) Index	237.37	LONDON
FTA World ex. UK (£) Index	232.77	LONDON
UK Government Securities Index	96.58	LONDON

Fig. 3. Cont/d.

40

payments in a year, although some companies pay four dividends in a year.

If you are on an advisory basis, the stockbroker would offer any advice on possible changes at the time of these valuations, or at any time in between.

If you are on a discretionary basis, the stockbroker will carry out transactions on his or her own initiative, and report to you. The effects of these changes will be shown on the periodical valuation.

If you are on an execution only basis, the stockbroker will only carry out transactions when you ask.

Being wary

Some people are wary of giving a stockbroker control of their investments. They may be aware of the security aspect. If a stockbroker holds your portfolio on a discretionary basis, it will be held in a nominee company. There are strict rules governing these nominee companies, and the stockbrokers will have to pay a considerable amount of money as a security bond. This guarantees the investments of the investors.

The other concern some people feel is that stockbrokers may carry out transactions unnecessarily. These transactions, they fear, would not enhance their portfolio, but only generate extra commission for the stockbroker. This practice is called 'churning'. The allusion is easy to see. The client's portfolio is like milk, being churned to produce butter for the stockbroker. However, this practice is extremely rare, especially amongst reputable brokers. If you suspect a broker of this, you can report it to the regulatory body. If found guilty, the stockbroker faces suspension.

UNDERSTANDING THE INDEX

When we talk of 'the index' we are talking of one of the indices published by the *Financial Times*. The most commonly quoted is the FTSE 100 share index. This is an index of the prices of the one hundred biggest companies quoted on the London Stock Exchange. The change in the index gives a measure of how share prices have moved.

There are however several other important indices, all published by the *Financial Times*. They include the 250 index, the All Share index, the Ordinary Share index, the Non-Financials index, the UK

Government Securities index, and the FT World index. These measure the price movements of shares in the different sectors.

The movements of these indices are often shown on graphs, with the familiar peaks and troughs. They provide a basis for comparison with the performance of other prices. For example, the price of any one share could be plotted on a graph, and then compared with the FTSE 100 index. This shows whether that share has performed better or worse than the average of the top one hundred. This comparison is often resorted to in considering the performance of unit trusts or investment trusts.

The indices are also sometimes used to show a correlation between share prices and other indicators, such as interest rates.

READING THE PRICES

Prices of shares are quoted each day in newspapers. The most complete list of prices is in the *Financial Times*. Other broadsheets also quote prices of most shares, and some tabloids also give prices of some of the most commonly traded shares. Figure 4 shows a typical day's price list in the financial press. Part of the list only is shown, for obvious reasons.

WATER			52 week		Market	Yield	
	Price	+ or –	High	Low	Capitalisation £ million	Gross	P/E
Anglian	709	+13	727	523	1911	6.1	9.5
Severn Trent	935	–12	1085	663	1250	5.0	10.3
CHEMICALS							
BOC	951	+1	1195	850	4750	3.5	16.4
Croda	445	+5	445	246	565	2.6	18.7

Fig. 4. Share prices listing.

The following information can be gleaned from the listings:

- Notes. These symbols are explained in the *Financial Times Guide to the London Share Service*. Some notes indicate that the *Financial Times* issues a service on this company. They provide reports on the companies, and free copies of the annual report.

- Price. This is the middle price at the close of trading, and given in pence.

- + or −. This shows how the price has moved since the end of the previous day's trading.

- 52 week high/low. This shows the maximum and minimum prices that the shares have reached in the previous year.

- Market capitalisation £m. This shows the value, in millions of pounds, of the total shares in issue, multiplied by the price. This gives an idea of how big the company is.

- Yield gross. This is the actual return you would receive on your money if you invested in the shares on the day of the report.

- P/E. This is the price/earnings ratio. It is a key indicator in deciding about investment in a company. The price of the share is expressed in relation to the earnings per share. The earnings per share is the profit of the company as a whole divided by the number of shares in issue.

PICKING A WINNER

Knowing how the stock market works is one thing. What you really need to know, however, is which companies to invest in.

Blue chips

This term relates to the top companies in the country. They are usually the ones in the FTSE 100 index. They represent the companies with the soundest track record, and the strongest financial base. All companies are engaged in a business of some kind, and these are the companies which have soundly based businesses. This is not to say that things could never go wrong. There have been spectacular failures of blue chip companies in the past.

So what factors do you look for in choosing an investment in shares?

Market sectors

You will see that the share prices quoted are divided into different sectors. These represent the types of businesses. Therefore, if you want to invest in a certain part of the economy (say, banking or leisure), you can see which quoted companies are in that sector.

It is also often more relevant to compare shares in one sector with others in that sector, rather than with other shares in different sectors, or with the market as a whole.

Price/earnings ratio

This is the relationship between the price of the share and the earnings of the company (i.e. its profit). For these purposes the earnings of the company as a whole are divided by the number of shares in issue to give the earnings per share.

Example

A company has profits of £3 million. It has ten million shares in issue. Its earnings per share are 30p. If the price quoted for that share is £3, then the price/earnings ratio is ten. This means that the price of the share represents ten years' profit. You would then compare this ratio with the market as a whole, or with the sector in which the company operates.

Quality of earnings

If the price/earnings ratio is based on historic figures, the information is not so relevant as future earnings. Of course, the problem is that future earnings are not a known figure, whereas historic earnings are known.

The price/earnings ratio, in fact, is governed largely by 'market sentiment'. This means what the analysts employed by stockbrokers think of the company. If they have doubts about the future prospects of the company and in particular its ability to maintain the profit levels, then the quality of earnings is said to be low.

Dividend yield

This is also a key indicator. It represents the actual rate of return you would get if you invested in the company at the price quoted. The rate of dividend per share is based on an amount per share. The actual rate you would receive depends on the price of the share.

Example

A company declares a dividend of 5 pence per share, as the only dividend for the year. The nominal value of the share is 25 pence, so the rate of return would appear to be 20%. However, that is not relevant for these purposes. If the price of the share were £1, then the dividend yield would be 5%, because you would receive 5 pence income for every £1 you invested.

Earnings growth

This is a measure of how the company's performance has improved or otherwise. If the earnings per share of a company have shown a steady growth, then the company has obviously improved its performance year on year. If there is a dip for one year in an otherwise steady increase, there may well be a good reason. If the earnings per share show a steady decline, you would want to find out why before investing in it.

OTHER MARKETS

The London Stock Exchange is the principal market for dealing in company shares in the UK. To qualify for inclusion, a company must satisfy certain strict requirements. However, there are other regional markets, and other markets in London.

The Alternative Investment Market and the Unlisted Securities Market (the AIM and the USM respectively) deal in a smaller number of companies' shares, and the quantity of deals in the shares is much less than the London Stock Exchange. If you have an investment in a company on the AIM, or the USM, therefore, it may not be as easy to sell the shares, simply because there may not be any, or a sufficient number, of buyers.

SPREADING THE RISK

Here is the fifth **Golden Rule of Investing**:

5. Do not put all your eggs in one basket.

Collective investments work on the principle of reducing risk by allowing you to invest in many different companies. If you do not have much money, you cannot have a wide variety of shares or other investments.

Collective investments work on the principle of a large number of people investing a relatively small amount into one 'pot' (which we shall call 'the fund') and then using that fund to invest in a larger range of investments than each individual could do alone. The risk is spread and the fund managers are able to manage the fund actively, to achieve the best results.

There are several forms of **collective investment.** The most common are:

- unit trusts
- investment trusts
- OEICs
- investment clubs.

Unit trusts

These are funds which accept money from new investors, and create new units in the total fund when new money is invested. When units are cashed in, those units are cancelled from the fund. The fund is set up as a trust, and trustees have oversight of the fund. Managers do the actual management of the fund. There are over 150 authorised unit trust groups in the UK and most of them manage many different funds. So there are thousands of funds to choose from.

The individual funds are usually targeted at particular sectors. For example, there are growth funds, income funds, high income funds, extra high income funds, American funds, blue chip funds, emerging market funds, Pacific funds and so on. The list is not quite endless, but almost.

Legally, a unit trust is governed by a trust deed. This creates a trust between the trustees (i.e. the people who are entrusted to safeguard the money) and the managers. Strictly speaking the fund is not owned by the investors, but by the trustees for the benefit of the investors.

How it works

When a unit trust receives new money from an investor, it creates new units in the fund. When an investor wishes to cash in his investment, the unit trust pays out the money and cancels the units. This is the main difference between unit trusts and investment trusts. This feature means that it is an 'open-ended fund'.

The price of units in each fund is quoted daily in the financial press and in the financial pages of daily newspapers. The prices are updated daily. The prices are arrived at by totalling the values of all the shares owned by the fund, and dividing that between the number of units in issue. This is another difference between unit trusts and investment trusts.

Question

What if I have shares, and want to invest instead in unit trusts?

Answer

Many unit trusts will accept shares in lieu of payment, provided that the shares are already on their investment list. The shares are taken in by the unit trust at their market value, with no deduction for dealing expenses, and an equivalent value of the units is credited to you. This can be an economic way of getting in to unit trusts from shares.

Investment trusts

These are limited liability companies, and are quoted on the Stock Exchange. They have a limited capital, and if you wish to buy shares in an investment trust company you have to buy them on the Stock Exchange. This means, in effect, that you are buying the shares from somebody else. This feature means that it is a 'closed fund'. It also means that you as a shareholder are the legal owner of a proportion of the company's assets.

The investment trust company itself invests in other companies, in much the same way that unit trusts do. Usually, however, the investment trust company does not act as an 'umbrella' with several funds. Each investment trust company has its own investment strategy, and invests within its plan.

Investment trusts are quoted companies on the Stock Exchange. The price of the shares is determined in the same way as prices of other shares – that is, by supply and demand. Thus the total value of their shares can be arrived at by multiplying the price by the total number of shares in issue. This is known as the market capitalisation.

By comparing this with the market value of all the shares which the company owns (its investments), you can arrive at a generally used indicator for investment trusts. It is usual in present conditions to find that the shares of investment trust companies stand at a discount to the value of the shares it holds as investments. The amount of this discount is an indicator of market sentiment towards the investment trust.

OEICs

This abbreviation stands for 'Open Ended Investment Companies'. As its name suggests, it combines the open-ended nature of unit trusts with the company legal structure of investment trusts.

A particular feature of OEICs is that prices are given as one price for buyers or sellers. This contrasts with both unit trusts and investment trusts, where there is a price spread between the price to a buyer and the price to a seller.

Investment clubs

As the name suggests, this is a more informal type of collective investment. It consists of a number of people getting together (usually on a regular basis) to make their investment plans. Obviously, as the number of people involved is much smaller, there is not so much money to invest and the members are usually amateurs. However, it does give the members more direct say in the investment of their money. Also, it provides a social occasion.

Because money is involved, it is necessary to have rules and a proper control system to safeguard the money and investments.

The development of the Internet has also seen the emergence of informal 'investment clubs' on the net. These are more informal, because the club members only exchange information and tips, rather than pooling their money.

CHOOSING A COLLECTIVE INVESTMENT

You are now ready to make an investment in a collective fund. What is available to you, and how should you decide? There are many sectors of funds available, but basically they fall within the following main categories:

- growth funds
- income funds
- high income funds
- geographical funds
- ethical funds
- split capital funds
- small companies funds
- tracker funds
- fund of funds
- gilt and fixed interest funds
- tax protected funds
- corporate bond funds.

What do they mean?

What is the investment bias or aim of each type of fund? Most of them are fairly obvious from their titles, but here is a brief summary:

Growth funds
These are slanted towards capital growth rather than income. They therefore provide a lower income than you might otherwise expect, and can be considered a slightly higher risk profile than income funds.

Income funds
These are geared to produce an income which has a realistic possibility of growing each year to at least keep pace with inflation. The income would normally be expected to approximate to the yield on the shares making up the FTSE 100 index. In practice, many fund managers actually do better than this, and the income is often higher than the FTSE 100 yield. In theory the capital growth potential should not be so good on these funds, but in practice, historically they have proved to have a good capital growth record.

High income funds
These are geared to produce a higher than average income, but this will not have as realistic a chance of increasing each year in line with inflation as pure income funds. The additional income is generated by mixing with ordinary shares, various fixed interest investments in the form of Government stocks, preference shares, debentures, etc. Obviously, the opportunities for capital growth are much more restricted.

Geographical funds
As the name implies, these funds invest in a particular area of the globe. Typical funds might be 'Far East', 'American', 'Pacific', 'European', 'Eastern European', or 'Emerging Markets'. These funds should be considered as a higher risk, and you should approach them with only as much confidence as you have in the economies of those geographical areas. If you do not know enough, or are not willing to trust an adviser implicitly, you would be better advised to stay away from these funds. Otherwise, any news broadcast could cause you great anxiety, as you see what is happening all over the world.

Ethical funds
We will look at these in some more depth in a later chapter. Suffice it to say that they are funds which either avoid certain negative factors, or which actively invest in certain positive factors. These are funds for true believers.

Split capital funds
These are funds in which the units or shares are in two classes – income or capital. One class gets all the capital growth, the other class gets all the income. This obviously gives a higher capital growth to capital shares or units, and higher income to income shares or units than would otherwise be the case.

Small companies funds
These may also sometimes be called 'Opportunity Funds'. They invest in smaller companies which the managers believe have good growth opportunities. Again, it is self-evident that they are a higher risk investment, but carry the opportunity for high capital growth.

Tracker funds
These are funds that 'track' the movement of various stock market indices. They do this by investing in the same companies as the companies whose shares are included in the index concerned. Thus, there are funds for example tracking the FTSE 100 index, the FTSE All Share index, the Dow Jones index, the Nikkei index, the Hang Seng index, and so on.

These funds therefore do not rely on active trading by the managers, since the investments are relatively stable and unchanging. Investments are only bought or sold when there is any change to the investments included on an index. In the recent past, for instance, when some of the larger building societies demutualised and became companies, they were included on the FTSE 100 index, and tracker fund managers had to adjust their holdings.

Otherwise, there is so little active management that the annual management fee on these funds is usually considerably lower than other types of funds. Many people invest in them for this reason, and because they have little faith in investment managers 'beating' the major indices.

Fund of funds
These funds invest in other unit trusts or investment trusts. This spreads the investment risk even further, and can be considered an even lower risk investment. However, because of the wide spread of investments, the income performance is not usually spectacularly good.

Gilt and fixed interest funds
These funds, as the name indicates, are invested in government

securities and other fixed interest stocks. They provide a spread of risk for those who wish to obtain the best fixed interest returns available.

Tax protected funds
These include Individual Savings Accounts, which provide a tax-free environment for income and capital gains. A maximum of £7,000 per person may be invested in these until 5th April 2001. Personal Equity Plans were also in this category before they were taken off the market. Investments within Personal Equity Plans may, however, still be traded or switched.

Corporate bond funds
These funds are invested in company fixed interest borrowings, such as bonds and debentures. They are most common in Individual Saving Account products. They offer investors a high return tax free income (when in an ISA) but very limited capital growth.

CHECKLIST

- Invest in the stock market through a broker.
- Find a broker you can trust.
- Choose between advisory, execution only, or discretionary.
- Read the prices and the index.
- Know how to pick a winner.
- Be aware of other markets.
- Spread the risk by using collective investments.
- Use a unit trust, an investment trust, an OEIC, or join an investment club.
- Choose the type of trust you want, and invest in one or a selection of trusts.

CASE STUDIES

Charles
Charles would like to invest some of his money directly into shares on the stock market. He finds a stockbroker through a work

colleague and goes to see him. He listens to the advice, and makes an investment in a selection of shares recommended by the stock-broker, on an advisory basis. At first he anxiously scans the prices almost every day, and worries when they dip. He later learns not to worry about smaller day-to-day fluctuations, but he still likes to keep abreast of things, and takes a newspaper with a regular financial section and 'city' report.

Derek chooses unit trusts

Derek is in his forties, and has inherited just over £25,000 from a relative. He decides he would not like to invest directly in the Stock Exchange, mainly because it has a mystique which he does not understand. However, he would like to invest in British industry and business. He decides that he would like to use unit trusts as they have a more approachable image. He invests in growth funds, to build up his capital, with a view to transferring to income funds when he retires.

Derek puts £7,000 in an ISA and then £5,000 into each of three other growth funds, with different unit trusts. This makes a total of £22,000 invested. He keeps the remaining £3,000 in a 'rainy day' account. He plans to transfer a further £5,000 each year into an ISA as long as they are available.

PERSONAL EVALUATION

1. What proportion (if any) of your capital do you think you should invest in collective investments?

2. How would you feel about having to cash in other investments to put money in collective investments?

3. At what point would you decide to invest directly into the stock market?

4. How would you decide what service to have from a stockbroker?

4

Other Investments

INVESTING IN YOUR COUNTRY

'As safe as the Bank of England' is a phrase that denotes absolute security. Certainly there is a place in everybody's savings or investment plans for secure investments backed by the government. These days there is quite a wide choice, so most people should be able to find something which meets their needs.

GOVERNMENT STOCKS

Just as companies need to raise money by borrowing from the public, so does the government. They do this by issuing stocks, most of which have a fixed repayment date, and a fixed rate of interest. This is a really low-risk form of investment, and is used by many people for just that feature. For this reason they are often referred to as **Gilts**. Many people with a portfolio of other investments also include a proportion of money in government stocks.

They are referred to under a series of names, including the following:

- Treasury stock
- Exchequer stock
- Consols (short for consolidated stock)
- Funding stock
- Convertible stock
- War loan.

Whatever name they bear, they are basically the same – by investing in them, you are lending the government money.

They are also quoted on the Stock Exchange, and for those purposes they are divided into:

- short dated (up to 5 years)
- medium dated (5 to 15 years)

- long dated (over 15 years)
- undated
- index linked.

The short, medium, and long dates refer to the redemption date. Undated stocks have no redemption date, and in theory could go on for ever. There are only three of these stocks currently in issue.

The stocks are **redeemed at par** (apart from the index linked stocks). That is to say, the repayment of the amount loaned is made on the stated date, at the same nominal amount at which they were issued. This may not be the same as the amount you paid, since their value fluctuates on the stock market according to the prevailing rates of interest.

Index linked stocks are ones which have a redemption date, but they are not repaid at par. The amount at which they are repaid is linked to the change in the retail prices index between the issue date and the redemption date.

Example
If an index linked stock was issued when the retail prices index stood at 100, and then repaid when the index stood at 200, the amount repaid would be twice the original nominal amount of the stock.

Because there is this inbuilt gain in the capital (in theory, the index could actually be lower at redemption, but this possibility is so remote as to be out of the reckoning), the interest rate paid on these stocks is relatively low. Of the index linked stocks in issue at present, the interest rates range between 2.5% and 4.375%.

Interest
Interest is paid twice yearly on government stocks. It is paid with income tax deducted at source. If you are not liable to tax, you may apply to the Inland Revenue to have the tax refunded.

Buying government stocks on the National Savings Register
As an alternative to buying government stocks on the Stock Exchange, you may buy them from National Savings. There is a small charge for this, but it is not usually as much as buying them on the Stock Exchange. The other main advantage of buying them this way is that the interest is paid gross – i.e. with no income tax deducted. However, the interest is taxable. This is often the preferred option for those whose income level means that they are not liable to income tax. The vast majority of government stocks are

on the National Savings Register and available to buy in this way.

Prices of government stocks
Government stocks are quoted on the Stock Exchange, and the price is quoted as a figure for which you may buy or sell £100 worth of the nominal value of the stock. See Figure 5 for a daily listing.

SHORTS (under 5 years)						
		52 weeks			Interest	Re-demption
	Price	High	Low	+ or –		Yield
Yield						
Treasury 8% 2000	103	104	102	+ 1	7.7	6.49
Convertible 9% 2000	104	106	103		8.6	6.5
MEDIUMS (5 to 15 years)						
Treasury 9% 2008	122	124	106	+ 1	7.33	6.04
Convertible 9% 2011	126	127	109		7.12	6.08

Fig. 5. Listing of government stock prices.

Thus, any particular stock can be priced over 100, in which case it is said to be at a premium, or under 100, when it is said to be at a discount. The price is governed by the prevailing interest rates at the time. For example, if prevailing interest rates are around 8%, and the nominal interest rate on a stock is 12%, the demand for that stock is likely to be high, and the price will rise above 100. In fact, in this case, unless the stock had a very short life to redemption, the price would rise to about 150, so that the yield would be roughly equivalent to the prevailing rates.

Yields
The financial press, in quoting prices for government stocks, gives yield figures. This means, as we have seen, the actual return which you will get on your money, and unless the price is 100, it will be different from the nominal interest rate of the stock. However, there are two yields quoted, an interest yield and a redemption yield.

Interest yield
The interest yield is the actual yield which you would receive on your money if you invested. This is simple to see, as in the example given above. If a stock with a nominal interest rate of 12% is quoted at 150, the interest yield will be 8%.

Redemption yield

The redemption yield is an additional indicator. It can be calculated because government stocks have a fixed redemption date (therefore it is not quoted for undated stocks). It represents the 'real' yield you would get over the remaining life of the stock. In other words, it takes into account the premium or the discount in the price.

I have called this the 'real' yield, because it is important to bear this factor in mind when comparing prices and yields. It is shown at its most extreme in very short-dated stocks. For example, in July 1997 the following price appeared in the financial press:

Exchequer 15% 1997 – price 102.5 – interest yield 14.63% – redemption yield 6.62%.

Therefore, with the price at 102.5, it might have appeared a good bargain to buy a 15% stock. However, the stock was dated 1997, and only had a few months to go before redemption – in fact, there was only one more half-yearly interest payment due. This meant also that in a few months' time the stock for which you had paid 102.5 would be redeemed at par – i.e. at 100.

In fact, as you would expect, the redemption yields of stocks with similar life spans are very similar, even though the interest yield may be quite different.

NATIONAL SAVINGS

National Savings are also a government department, and once again when you invest in National Savings you are lending money to the government. National Savings have several different products. These are:

- National Savings Bank Ordinary Accounts
- National Savings Bank Investment Accounts
- National Savings Certificates
- Premium Bonds
- National Savings Income Bonds
- National Savings Capital Bonds
- National Savings Pensioners Guaranteed Income Bonds
- National Savings Fixed Rate Savings Bonds

● National Savings Children's Bonus Bonds.

Each of these have different features, as follows:

National Savings Bank
This is, as the name implies, a savings bank which operates through all post offices. The only accounts available are the following two.

National Savings Bank Ordinary Accounts
This is a savings account which gives a low rate of interest (at the time of writing this was 1.25% on balances up to £500, and 1.35% on balances from £500 upwards). There is a minimum investment of £20, and a maximum of £10,000. The interest is variable, paid gross, and the first £70 per year of interest is tax free.

National Savings Bank Investment Accounts
This is a savings account which requires one month's notice for withdrawals. It gives higher rates of interest than the ordinary account (at the time of writing, variable up to 5.1%). There is a minimum investment of £20, and a maximum of £100,000. Higher rates of interest are paid on balances over £500. The interest is variable, paid gross, but is liable to tax.

National Savings Certificates
There are fixed interest certificates and index linked certificates.

Fixed Interest Certificates
These are certificates issued by the National Savings office. You buy certificates in any amount from £100 to £10,000. The interest is guaranteed for the five-year term of the certificate. The interest is also free of tax. However, you may not draw on the interest before the five-year term is finished. If you do need to cash in the certificates before the five-year term, the interest rate is lower for the earlier years. If you do not cash in the certificates at the end of the five-year term, they continue to earn interest, but only at a variable rate called the 'General Extension Rate'. This is lower than the normal rate on certificates.

Index Linked Certificates
These certificates are also issued for five-year terms, and again you may invest from £100 to £10,000. The value at the end of the five-year term is calculated in two parts.

One part is the index linked part. This means that the certificate's value increases by the increase in the retail prices index over the five-year period.

The other part is the interest. Interest is given at a lower rate than the fixed interest certificates, and added to the value at the end of the five-year term.

If you need to cash in early, the index linking applies after the first anniversary of the purchase, and interest is also added from that date, but at a lower rate. If you do not cash in the certificates at the end of the five-year term, they continue to earn index linked 'extension terms', which are lower than the current rate on new issues.

Premium Bonds

You may invest a minimum of £100 to a maximum of £20,000 in Premium Bonds. They do not pay interest, but once you have held the Bonds for a full calendar month your number goes into the prize draw.

There is one prize of £1 million every month, and a number of other prizes from £50 to £100,000. Each £1 unit has a fixed chance of 19,000 to 1 of winning a prize every month. The size of the prize fund determines how many prizes of each denomination there are (except the 'jackpot' prize of £1 million, one of which is guaranteed every month). The prize fund is determined by a notional rate of interest on the total value of Premium Bonds in issue.

The Bonds may be cashed in at any time without notice, at the same value for which they were purchased. The prizes are exempt from tax.

National Savings Income Bonds

You may invest a minimum of £500 up to a maximum of £1,000,000 in Income Bonds. They pay monthly interest at a variable rate, and the interest is paid gross – i.e. without deduction of income tax. The interest is taxable. The interest rate is fairly competitive, and a higher rate of interest applies for investments of £25,000 or more. Three months' notice is required for withdrawal, although you may cash them in without notice, but with a penalty equivalent to 90 days' interest.

National Savings Capital Bonds

You may invest a minimum of £100 up to a maximum of £250,000 in Capital Bonds. This is a lump sum investment with a fixed term of five years, and a fixed, guaranteed interest rate for the whole five-year term. However, the interest rate is 'tiered'. This means that the interest starts at a lower figure for the first year, then increases each year to make up the full guaranteed amount at the end of the five-year term.

The interest is not paid to you, but added to the amount of the Bond. National Savings send you a statement every year to show how the Bond has grown with the added interest. The interest is added gross, and the amount of the interest is taxable. You may cash in the Bond at any time without notice. Repayment is then made of the amount standing to your credit at the previous anniversary of the purchase, plus interest from then at the rate of interest for the last year. Thus, early cashing in means that you lose out on the full interest rate.

National Savings Pensioners' Guaranteed Income Bonds
You must be over 60 years of age to buy these Bonds. You may invest a minimum of £500, up to a maximum of £1,000,000 in these Bonds. There are five year bonds and two year bonds.

The interest is at a guaranteed fixed rate for the term. Interest is paid monthly, and is paid gross. However, it is taxable.

You may cash in these Bonds early, but at 60 days' notice, and during the notice period no interest is paid. Alternatively, you may cash them in without notice, but subject to a penalty of 90 days' interest on the amount withdrawn.

National Savings Fixed Rate Savings Bonds
You may invest a minimum of £500 and a maximum of £1,000,000 in these Bonds. Interest is paid monthly or annually, at a guaranteed rate for a period, but with tax deducted at source.

These Bonds are offered with four different fixed terms, of six months, one year, eighteen months, or three years. The rate of interest depends on the term you choose, and the rate is tiered, with different rates for investments from £500 up to £20,000, from £20,000 up to £50,000, and over £50,000.

The Bonds are held for their full term, then National Savings will tell you what your options are at the completion of the term.

National Savings Children's Bonus Bonds
These may be opened by anyone over the age of 15, for anyone under that age. The minimum investment is £25, and the maximum £1,000. These figures are for each person on whose behalf the investment is

made. Thus, a parent may put in up to £1,000 for each of their children, or any other children. The bonds are controlled by the child's parent or legal guardian, irrespective of who made the actual investment of money.

Interest is at a fixed, guaranteed rate for five years. At the end of the five-year term a bonus is added to the investment. This bonus is also fixed and guaranteed at the outset. The interest and the bonus are exempt from income tax.

When interest rates are changed, a new issue of these Bonds is made. At that point a new investment may be made in the new issue on top of what has already been invested.

These Bonds may be cashed in early without notice, but again there is a loss of interest. Repayment will be made of the amount of the Bond at the previous anniversary, plus interest at a daily rate up to the time of cashing in. Bonuses are not paid until the full five-year term is finished. The Bond may also be cashed in on the child's 21st birthday.

When you are in retirement, these can be useful for giving to grandchildren.

USING LIFE ASSURANCE AS AN INVESTMENT

Whole life policies

Life assurance in its simplest and purest form is a means of protection. You pay a regular premium, each month or each year, and when you die your dependants get a lump sum which will be of help to them. There has to be an 'insurable interest'. This means that you cannot just take out a life assurance policy on somebody unconnected to you – say the President of the United States, and then collect a lump sum when he dies. It has to be somebody whose death would otherwise cause you loss. This is most commonly a family member, but it can be a key person in your business whose death would cause a financial loss.

This type of policy is known as a 'whole life' policy. Cover is provided throughout the life of the person insured, provided the premiums are paid. It can also cover the lives of two people, usually husband and wife. It is then known as a 'joint life' policy.

Term policies

Life assurance policies can be indefinite, or for a fixed term. A term policy would be taken out because the protection is only needed for a certain length of time – for example, during the period of repaying a mortgage.

A level term policy is one in which the amount of the cover stays the same for the whole term of the policy. A decreasing term policy is one in which the cover decreases year by year. This type of policy is often used in conjunction with repayment mortgages, where the balance on the mortgage account decreases each year, and the policy provides cover which broadly matches the decreasing balance.

Endowment policies

A development of the simple 'protection' type policy was the endowment policy. This added a savings element on to the protection element. The premiums are of course higher for this sort of policy. The key feature is that they cover a definite period (the term), during which your life would be insured for a certain sum, but at the end of the term, (known as the maturity), if you are still alive you receive a lump sum. The most common type of endowment policy is a 'with profits' policy. This means that the amount paid in each year is invested by the insurance company, and part of the profits each year are added to the value of the policy which is paid out at maturity.

This is done by the insurance company declaring 'reversionary bonuses' each year which are added to the value of the policy. These bonuses cannot be deducted once they have been added. Reversionary bonuses do not tend to suffer the extremes of fluctuations that other 'unit linked' policies do. This is because the bonuses are subject to a 'rolling average' adjustment. This ensures that large fluctuations in the value of the underlying investments are smoothed out, and a more level bonus is added each year. Then, at the maturity, a 'terminal bonus' is added. The terminal bonus is not guaranteed. The terminal bonus tends to fluctuate more than the reversionary bonus, because it is more affected by the actual increase or decrease in the value of the underlying investments of the particular year in which the terminal bonus is added.

Unitised policies

Some endowment policies are unitised. That means that the premiums buy units in the with profits fund. The unit prices increase as the bonus is added on a daily basis. At the maturity of the policy, the value of the units plus a terminal bonus is paid out.

Endowment mortgages

A relatively recent development has been the combination of endowment policies with mortgages. The amount of the mortgage is covered by taking out an endowment policy for the term of the mortgage. Then, the repayments to the mortgage lender are of interest only. At the maturity of the endowment policy the mortgage is paid off with the maturity proceeds of the policy. The protection element is provided by this policy as well as the investment element.

In practice, these policies have been taken out with the prospect of the maturity sum covering not just the repayment of the mortgage but also an additional sum. However, these policies are at the mercy of the bonus rates declared. In recent years, some shorter term policies have not always covered the full outstanding amount of the policy, because the bonuses have been insufficient.

Bonds

Another relatively recent development has been the 'Insurance Bond'. This is in effect a single premium endowment assurance policy, if it has a fixed term. If it continues until death then it is an open-ended, whole of life policy. The fixed term is often five or ten years.

Income bonds

In return for a single premium paid 'up front' you receive a fixed income each year, and the return of the premium, sometimes with some increase added, at the end of the term. Because of tax regulations, these can be advantageous in certain cases.

Capital growth bonds

The single premium is paid 'up front', but instead of the income being paid out it 'rolls up' in the policy to provide a larger sum on maturity.

Commission

As with all insurance policies, if they are sold to you by tied agents or independent advisers, they may be subject to commission being paid. The effect of this is particularly noticeable with bonds. The effect of the initial commission may be that if you wanted to withdraw the money in the early years, you might suffer a loss. Always check this before you invest.

Trading endowment policies

If you found that you could not keep up the premiums on

endowment policies, in the past the only thing to do was to surrender them to the insurance company. You could get back a certain amount, depending on the number of years you had been paying the premiums. However, the amount would always be at a large discount to the true value of your fund.

In recent years, a market has grown up in traded endowment policies. This means that instead of simply surrendering your endowment policy to the insurance company, you could sell them to another person who would continue to pay the premiums, and then collect the funds at maturity. In general, this method produces a larger amount than surrendering the policy.

Buying traded endowment policies (TEPs) has also been seen as an investment tool. A person buying such a policy takes over the liability for the remaining premiums, and the policy continues on the life of the original person who sold the policy. The amount paid for the policy depends on several factors, of which the most obvious is the remaining time left until maturity. The earlier death of the original life assured would of course mean an earlier maturity.

This type of investment is fairly complex, and needs the advice of the market makers, of whom there are several specialising in this area. However, it is a relatively low risk investment, since the minimum value of the policy usually corresponds very closely to the purchase price and premiums paid. Then at maturity there is a relatively large amount added as terminal bonus.

Once again, however, the amount of the final benefit is at the mercy of the bonuses. In recent years annual bonuses have fallen. In some cases the terminal bonus is also lower, and the overall return for a purchased endowment policy could be disappointing.

CHECKLIST

- Government stocks and National Savings products are a low-risk form of investment. Some are dated, some are index linked. There is a wide range to choose from; some are only available to restricted classes of people.

- Use whole of life and term assurance for protection.

- Endowment policies, sometimes connected to mortgages, can be a good investment over the long term.

- Bonds can be tax efficient in some cases.

- Traded endowment policies can give you more money if you need to surrender the policy, but beware if buying – the bonuses may be disappointing in the short term.

CASE STUDIES

Alison

Alison has always had a National Savings account and some Premium Bonds, which her parents started for her when she was a child. She keeps these open, not with any serious amounts of money, but just for the sake of keeping them open. And who knows, she may come up trumps with her Premium Bonds.

Alison considers the benefits of an endowment mortgage when she gets a mortgage. She likes the idea of saving in this way. As she is still fairly young, the cost of this type of policy is not great. She has also considered the idea of a pension mortgage, but rejected this. She is not sure at this stage of how long her working life might be, and how long she might take out of a career to raise a family.

Charles

Being of the right age, Charles decides to put some money into Pensioners' Guaranteed Income Bonds. These give a high rate of interest, and it is guaranteed for five years. He decides it will give a good mix with some other equity based investments.

PERSONAL EVALUATION

1. Do you feel any different about investing in your country to investing in a commercial enterprise?

2. Do you feel that investing in any of the index-linked investments allays your fears about inflation?

3. What proportion of your total money do you think you should put in gilts or National Savings products? Why?

4. Have you worked out how much you need to insure your life for? Have you regularly reviewed it?

5. Do you know if you would benefit from the tax treatment of bonds?

5

Unconventional Investing

There are a number of investment opportunities which are not 'conventional'. Many people fight shy of these, simply because they *are* unconventional. The real problem is a lack of understanding.

Here is the sixth **Golden Rule of Investing**:

> 6. Do not invest in anything unless you understand it.

Some years ago a large pension fund raised a few eyebrows because it invested in an 'old master' painting. In the event, it actually made a good profit for the pension fund. If you are thinking of being unorthodox in your investments, then:

- make sure you understand what you are investing in, and
- evaluate the risk factor.

There are many sorts of investments which could be considered as unorthodox, including:

- ethical investments
- collectables, including wines
- commodities
- derivatives.

ETHICAL INVESTMENTS

There is now a large choice of 'ethical funds'. If you are an investor with a conscience this gives you the chance to put your money where your mouth is. There are two main types of ethical investment – positive and negative.

Positive investments
Positive investments channel money into companies that promote a

certain ethical or 'green' agenda. These can include:

- energy and resource conservation
- recycling
- renewable energy
- pollution control
- free range foods
- sustainable agriculture and forestry
- minimising waste
- environmental technology
- public transport
- fair trade with third world countries.

Negative investments

Negative investments concentrate on avoiding companies which are involved in things such as:

- tobacco
- alcohol
- arms trade
- exploitation of third world countries
- heavy pollution
- animal testing
- pornography
- environmental damage.

Choosing an ethical investment

There are now many ISAs and unit trusts which allow you to choose the right type of ethical investment to suit your preferences. The good news is that most of the ethical funds perform at least as well as other funds in the same sector of the market. A recent survey of the FTSE 100 companies showed that the 'greenest' and 'most ethical' companies performed better than those at the other end of the scale. You do not need to suffer financially in order to exercise your conscience.

If you are going to invest ethically, the one question you need to ask yourself is: does it make sense to invest only part of my money in ethical investments? The logic of ethical investment is that all your money should be invested ethically if that is where your scruples lead you. To put it another way, ethical investment is not something you can 'dabble' in. If you only put a token amount in ethical investments, then the rest of your money is going into non-ethical investments.

Ethical saving

Saving with a bank or building society can also be done ethically. The main opportunities here are with the Co-operative bank, the Ecology building society, and Triodos bank.

- The Co-operative bank has two million customers, and does not deal with repressive regimes overseas, the fur trade, tobacco producers, field sports, or animal experiments for cosmetics.

- The Ecology building society specialises in lending money for socially responsible housing projects.

- The Triodos bank is a Dutch bank that has been in the UK since 1995. It invests in projects which add social or environmental value.

Some 'ethical' banks or building societies offer accounts which pay interest equivalent to the rate of inflation, and pass on profits to worthy causes.

- Remember that ethical investing does not mean low-risk investing.

COLLECTABLES

Most people at some point in their lives have had collections of things. It may be stamps, football programmes, teddy bears, dolls – in fact almost anything. There are many collectors who take these things seriously into adult life, and other sorts of collections are often only developed in adult life. These include such things as fine wines, antiquarian books, paintings etc.

There are many sorts of collections you could make if you have a mind to. Some which have established markets are:

- political memorabilia
- antique greetings cards
- sporting equipment and memorabilia
- Oriental ceramics
- carpets and rugs
- furniture
- toys
- film posters
- garden statuary
- stuffed animals and fish.

This is by no means a complete list, but it gives an idea of the range of things which could make collections, and for which a market exists.

In order to make an investment out of a collection, it does not take much apart from a serious dedication to it. However, collections are usually made primarily for pleasure. The investment potential should only be secondary. There are three main things to bear in mind when considering collectables.

Knowing your subject

Most collections come about through an interest in the items – often the interest is kindled as a child, and grows in adult life. In order to make a collection into a serious investment, you should know your subject well. It is no use collecting, say, fine wines, if you do not know which ones will improve when they are laid down and which will increase in value. But do not be put off by a mystique about any subject. If something interests you, learn more about it. You can become an enthusiast, and even an expert about your particular pet subject. Some collections may be built up by spending much time at car boot sales or the like. Others may need serious buying at auctions or specialist shops.

Keeping them safe

The one thing that is different about collectables is that they have an actual physical existence. That means that they need to be kept somewhere. Some items may need special storage conditions, such as a cool wine cellar. Some items, such as pictures, may need to be displayed and lit to be properly appreciated. Some items are even of such importance that they are loaned to a local or national museum for display. Many items will be of some value, and will therefore need to be protected. This may mean special anti-burglary precautions, and for any serious collection your normal household insurance will probably not cover it for loss or damage. You will probably have to incur extra cost in insuring it specifically.

Realising their value

Collections suffer from one obvious disadvantage – they do not produce an income. Therefore, in order to benefit from them in a financial sense you will have to realise their value in some way. This could mean having to part with something you have become attached to. Bear this in mind at the outset.

PLAYING THE MARKET

Anyone who has a portfolio of stocks and shares does a certain amount of buying and selling of shares. However, it is possible to make the buying and selling of stocks and shares a separate speculative activity. It is not so much the yield from dividends that is sought, but the profits to be had from trading the shares. If you do this consistently, the Inland Revenue can and will treat you as being in business as a **share trader**.

This form of speculation can be a high-risk area. The risk is obviously lowered if you have enough money to spread the risk by holding many different stocks and shares. Speculators are trying to anticipate the movement of the markets. This can mean spending much time reading the reports of analysts about various companies, or generally keeping up to date with market news (and market rumours). Not all speculators are short-term dealers. Some take a long-term view, and their stocks or shares are held a long time before being sold. To that extent, they are acting in the same way as traditional investors.

Charting for pleasure and profit

Chartists are people who look for patterns in the price movements of shares. These patterns are seen easily in charts or graphs of the price movements. The peaks and troughs form patterns which can be related to past experience to indicate that a price is about to peak, or has bottomed out. This indicates when to buy or sell. Chartists are therefore not concerned so much with the details of the economic reality of the company represented by those shares, but the actions of a wide spread of investors.

Perhaps the most well known expression of this is the Elliott wave principle, first propounded by R. N. Elliott in 1934, in the United States. It is based upon the patterns created by graphs of price movements. Although this may seem esoteric, the 'rules' derived from it have proved reliable. They do not claim to predict the future, but to provide a structure for analysis of the markets.

If you have time to devote to it, and a mathematical bent, it can be an interesting pursuit as well as an investment opportunity. Always remember, however, that this is still in the realms of speculative investment.

Day trading

Another form of speculative investment is **day trading**. This involves buying and selling investments on the same day, in the hope of making a profit. Because of the dealing charges, there has to be a large movement in the price of the investment to make this worthwhile. However, because trading all takes place on the same day, you do not need capital to do it.

Never lose sight of the precarious nature of this type of trading. It is reckoned that about 70% of those carrying out day trading make losses.

COMMODITIES

Commodities include products such as coffee, cocoa, rubber, metals of all sorts – in fact, the raw materials that are used in industrial and food production. Because many of these come from abroad, and the process time to get them to the finished products can be considerable, the businesses that buy and sell them like to hedge the prices. This has led to markets growing up in which investors and speculators can trade in the future prices of these commodities.

The dealings take place in highly regulated environments. Outside investors can only deal through brokers, and are essentially taking a gamble on the future prices of the commodities traded in. The amounts needed to trade in these futures are not inconsiderable, and it is a high-risk area.

DERIVATIVES

These are also known as **Options**, but the term **derivatives** can also embrace other things such as futures, contracts for differences, swaps, etc. They can appear complicated, and certainly it would normally be more sophisticated investors who deal in these. Remember – do not invest in anything unless you understand it. The essence of derivatives is that you have the opportunity to benefit (or lose) from an underlying 'position' (such as the movement in the price of a share) without complete 'exposure' to that position. In plain language that means you can benefit from an increase in a share price without actually owning the shares.

Options
The simplest form of derivative is the option. These are agreements by which you pay a price (known as the option premium) for the right to buy or sell shares at a fixed price within a certain time scale.

These agreements also limit the number of shares to be traded under the agreement.

If you do not exercise your option within the time scale, you have lost the rights under that agreement. The person to whom you paid the premium keeps the money. However, if you do exercise your right, the person to whom you paid the premium must fulfil his side of the bargain.

The types of options are:

- Calls – this gives the right to buy the shares.

- Puts – this gives the right to sell the shares.

- Doubles – this gives the right either to buy or to sell, but not both.

This form of trading is recognised on the London Stock Exchange and is called London's Traditional Options Market. Shares in any company quoted on the London Stock Exchange may be the subject of a traditional options contract.

There is another market dealing in 'Traded Options'. This is a separate market in which the options are for fixed numbers of shares, with fixed expiry patterns, and a fixed scale of exercise prices. On the Traded Options market, the options themselves can be traded, rather than the underlying shares, and the range of shares on which options are traded is rather more limited than on the London Stock Exchange.

Options could be considered low to medium risk in the sense that the only money at risk is the money you have paid for the option premium. This is only a fraction of the cost of holding the actual shares. However, the option premium itself is a high risk item, since the loss could be 100%.

CHECKLIST

- Ethical investments are:
  - positive or negative
  - available as PEPS or unit trusts
  - also found in banks or building societies
  - not necessarily low risk.

- Collectables are not just an investment, but also a leisure pursuit.

Make sure you know your subject, keep the collection safe and be prepared to realise its value.

- Commodities are:
  - speculation based on future pricing
  - high-risk.

- Dealing in stocks and shares and day trading is:
  - speculative trading
  - high-risk.

- Options are the simplest form of derivative which can be call, put or double. This form of trading is called London's Traditional Options Market and is part of the London Stock Exchange.

CASE STUDIES

Max

Max is a very wealthy, sophisticated investor. He is willing to put aside a relatively small part of his wealth to try some more speculative forms of investment. He dabbles in options and commodity trading. However, because he is only dabbling he loses heavily, and decides to stick to the things he understands better. Although he has lost money, he is wealthy and he had mentally resigned himself to the fact that he could lose the money before he even started.

PERSONAL EVALUATION

1. Are you in a position to set aside some wealth for more unorthodox investments?

2. Do you feel strongly enough about any ethical issues that you would invest in them?

3. Do you agree that you should invest 'all or nothing' in ethical investments?

4. Do you have any interest which could form the basis of a collection, and if so, could this form part of your investment strategy?

6

Getting State Benefits

There are many state benefits which apply particularly to retired people. It is important to understand how the Social Security system works, and how to claim the different benefits.

UNDERSTANDING THE SYSTEM

The Social Security system in this country is based upon people contributing to the system when they are in work (or voluntarily contributing if they wish to keep their contribution record up to date) and being able to claim the benefits when out of work, on low income, or retired.

Benefits can be:

- contributory or non-contributory
- dependent on your age or not
- means-tested by reference to your income and/or capital.

STATE RETIREMENT PENSION

You qualify for the state retirement pension when you reach the 'pension age' – i.e. at present 60 for women and 65 for men. This benefit is contributory, so if you have not made contributions you do not qualify for the benefit. You may have made contributions, but not up to the required amount. In this case, you will qualify for a reduced pension. All state retirement pensions are taxable under income tax.

The pension is made up of four parts:

- the basic pension
- additional pension
- graduated pension
- extra addition on reaching age 80.

Taxation

All of your state pension is taxable, except the extra Christmas bonus and the cold weather payments for fuel.

Basic pension

This is paid at a uniform rate to everyone who has fulfilled the contribution conditions. There are four different rates (the rates shown are weekly, and are the current rates at the time of writing):

- Single person   £67.50
- Wife – on husband's contributions   £40.40
- Married couple – on husband's contributions   £107.90
- Married couple (if both paid full contributions)   £135.00

Additional pension

The State Earnings Related Pension Scheme (SERPS) started in April 1978. Under this scheme, if you were employed from 6th April 1978 onwards, you will have paid National Insurance contributions on your earnings. As the name suggests, the contributions are related to your earnings, and the amount goes towards providing the additional pension.

The earnings between the 'lower earnings limit' (LEL) and the 'upper earnings limit' (UEL) are used as the basis on which the additional pension is calculated. The formula was based on 25% of the earnings between the specified levels until 1999, and gradually reduces to 20% from 2009. At the same time, there are plans to replace the SERPS with a new State Second Pension at some time at or after April 2002. However, any additional pension built up with SERPS will be protected.

It is possible to contract out of SERPS by joining an appropriate personal pension scheme or an occupational pension scheme run by your employer. As always, if you are considering this step, make sure you take independent advice.

Graduated pension

If you were employed between April 1961 and April 1975, you will have paid graduated National Insurance contributions. These were additional contributions, and they, like SERPS, entitle you to an additional pension.

Over 80 pension

This is non-contributory. When you reach age 80 you will receive an extra 25p per week on your pension. If you are receiving a retirement pension of less than the weekly amount paid to a wife on her husband's contributions, an over-80 pension will be paid to bring that pension up to that amount.

Going on working

Your state pension is not affected by any other income or earnings. Therefore you can go on working after you reach the pension age. However, if you are claiming an addition to your pension for a dependent wife or husband, that addition *will* be affected by the dependant's earnings.

If you go on working after pension age, you will receive a certificate of exception from the DSS, and you will not have to pay any National Insurance contributions. However, your employer will still have to go on paying the employer's contributions.

Deferring your pension

When you reach retirement age, you do not have to start drawing your pension immediately. You can defer the pension for up to five years. The effect of deferring the pension is that it increases by 1% for every seven weeks that you defer. Thus, if you deferred for a whole year, you would increase the pension by about 7.5%, and if you deferred for the full five years, you would increase the pension by about 37.5 per cent.

RETIRING EARLY

You may retire from work before the pension age. If so, you may claim the Jobseeker's Allowance. This benefit is made up of two elements. The contribution-based allowance is based on your National Insurance contributions record, and the income-based allowance is means-tested.

To claim the allowance you must be:

- under the pension age
- unemployed or working less than 16 hours per week
- capable of and available for work
- actively seeking work, by entering into a Jobseeker's Agreement.

The contribution-based allowance is:

- paid for a maximum of 26 weeks
- without any addition for dependants, and
- reduced if you have any occupational pension over £50 per week.

The income-based allowance can be paid:

- in addition to the contribution-based allowance, or
- on its own if:
  - you do not have sufficient contributions, or
  - you have received contributions-based allowances for 26 weeks.

The income-based allowance is broadly the same as Income Support, and it is means-tested by reference to your savings *and* your income. If you have a partner or spouse, the means test relates to the joint savings and income. In addition, the partner or spouse must be out of work, or working less than 24 hours per week on average. If you are over 60, or receiving Invalid Care Allowance, but would otherwise qualify for the income-based allowance, you should claim Income Support instead.

If you are receiving the income-based allowance, you are also entitled to other benefits such as Housing Benefit, Council Tax Benefit and help with NHS costs.

INCAPACITY

If you are unable to work because of sickness, you may be entitled to Incapacity Benefit. It is not means-tested, and it is contributions-based. Any new claimants from 6th April 2001 will have the benefit reduced if they have personal or occupational pensions of more than £85 per week.

There are three rates of benefit:

- short-term lower rate
- short-term higher rate
- long-term rate.

The short-term lower rate is payable for the first 28 weeks, if you are self-employed or unemployed. (If you are employed you will receive Statutory Sick Pay for that period.)

The short-term higher rate is payable from the 29th week to the 52nd week.

able after 52 weeks, and continues until

e is not taxable. The short-term higher rate
are taxable.

weeks you need to supply a medical certificate from
tor to state that you are unable to do your normal job.
ter 28 weeks (or if you do not have a job, the start of
pacity), you must undertake a 'personal capability assessment'.
involves a questionnaire and in some cases a medical
ination. This assessment decides whether you are incapable
y work – not just your normal job.

PROTECTING YOUR PENSION RIGHTS

If you are receiving either Jobseeker's Allowance or Incapacity
Benefit, your contributions record will be credited with weekly
contributions for each week that you draw those benefits. Therefore,
if you are under 60, it will be worth while 'signing on' even if you are
not entitled to the Jobseeker's Allowance. This will entitle you to
receive the credits. If you are a man aged between 60 and 64 you will
automatically receive those credits, even if you are not incapacitated
or unemployed. However, if you are abroad for more than six
months in any year, you will not be entitled to those credits.

Getting a pension forecast

You can write to the Benefits agency of the Department for Social
Security at Newcastle upon Tyne to request a pension forecast. This
will tell you how much retirement pension you are due to receive.
This will highlight if you have any deficiency in your contributions
record. If so, you can pay a lump sum to make up the deficiency, and
obtain full benefit. You may also pay voluntary contributions to
keep up your contributions record.

WIDOWS' BENEFITS

These benefits are for women who are widowed after the age of 55.
The benefit depends on the husband's contributions record.

The Widow's Payment

This is a tax-free lump sum of £1,000. It is paid if:

- a woman is widowed – under the age of 60, or
- she is over 60, provided that
  - the husband was under 65, or
  - the husband was over 65 but not receiving the State Retirement Pension.

The Widow's Pension

This is a taxable pension. It is paid:

- if a woman is widowed between the ages of 55 and 64, and
- she had not started to receive the State Retirement Pension.

If her husband did not have a full contribution record, she may not receive the full pension. She may get an Additional Pension based on her husband's earnings since April 1978.

On reaching age 60 you can elect to draw the State Retirement Pension or stay on Widow's pension until you reach 65. You should check with the Benefits Agency what is the most beneficial. There may be additional State Retirement Pension due to Graduated Pension Contributions. However, if you decide to continue with the Widow's Pension, you do not earn any extra Retirement Pension by this deferral of the Retirement Pension.

The Widow's Pension is not affected by any other earnings.

Remarrying

If you remarry before reaching 60, you will lose your Widow's Pension. If you live with someone as his wife, your Widow's Pension will be suspended.

If you are over 60 and receiving a Retirement Pension based on your late husband's contributions, you will not lose this pension if you remarry.

BEREAVEMENT BENEFITS

From April 2001, new benefits are to be introduced. These are available to anybody, man or woman, widowed after that date.

Bereavement Payment

The bereavement payment, which will be increased to £2,000, is payable to anybody widowed before the pension age (currently 60 for women, 65 for men). It will not be taxable.

Bereavement Allowance

This will be a weekly allowance, payable to anybody who is widowed after the introduction date. It will be at the same rate as the State Retirement Pension, but there will be no SERPS addition. It will be taxable, and it will only be payable for a maximum of 52 weeks. For the first five years extra help will be available, though this will be means-tested.

INCOME SUPPORT

This benefit is non-contributory, but means-tested. It is available to anybody, not just those at or near retirement. However, when applied to people over 60, it is called 'Minimum Income Guarantee'. If you qualify for this benefit, you probably also qualify for Housing Benefit and/or Council Tax Benefit. In fact, even if you do not qualify for this benefit, you could still qualify for the other two.

Other benefits are also available if you are on Income Support, including help towards glasses, free dental treatment and prescriptions, and possible grants from the Social Fund.

You qualify for Income Support if you meet the following requirements:

- You do not have more than £8,000 savings.

- You are on a low income.

- You are under 60, but do not need to 'sign on' (because you are ill or a carer), or you are over 60.

- You do not work 16 hours per week or more and your partner (if you have one) does not work 24 hours per week or more.

- You are not excluded from claiming benefit by your immigration status, and you are normally resident in the UK.

Income Support is calculated by reference to published figures which are reckoned as the minimum living standard. Any shortfall from your income (plus adjustments for your savings) to that figure is granted as Income Support, at a weekly rate.

Savings

Any savings over £3,000 mean that the 'minimum standard' figure is reduced by £1 per week for every £250 over that limit. If your savings are over £8,000, you do not qualify at all for Income Support.

Savings includes:

- cash

- bank and building society accounts

- National Savings accounts

- Premium Bonds

- stocks and shares

- property (other than your private dwelling)

- your share of any joint savings with other people.

The following are specifically excluded from savings:

- your own home

- the surrender value of a life assurance policy

- arrears of certain benefits

- your personal possessions.

If you are living with a spouse or partner, their savings are also counted towards the limits.

You cannot deliberately 'deprive' yourself of savings just to get round the savings limit. This would include such things as giving money to your family, or buying expensive or luxury items. You could be refused benefit because of this.

Low income

All income, earned or unearned, is counted towards the limit. For a couple, both partners' incomes are added together. For these purposes, some income is fully ignored, and some income is partly ignored.

Fully ignored
- Housing Benefit and Council Tax Benefit

- mobility and care components of Disability Living Allowance

- Attendance Allowance

- actual interest or income from savings up to £8,000

- the special War Widows' Pension introduced in 1990 for pre-1973 war widows

- payments from friends, relatives or charities towards things not covered by benefits (such as television costs, telephone, etc).

Partly ignored (weekly figures)
- £5 of earnings if you are single and you work part-time

- £10 of your or your partner's part-time earnings

- £15 of earnings if you are a carer and work part-time (this is instead of the £5 or £10 above)

- £10 of a War Widows or War Disablement Pension

- £20 of regular payments from a friend, relative or charity

- £4 of any payment by a subtenant living in your home (£13.25 if the payment includes heating)

- £20 income from a boarder plus half the boarder's charge over £20.

Minimum living standard figures
The figures are given as weekly amounts. At the time of writing, these are £52.20 for a single person, and £81.95 for a couple. In addition, various 'premiums' are added to these figures, and the ones that apply to people over 60 are as follows.

Pensioner premium
This is given to single people aged between 60 and 74, and to a couple, if both are under 75, and one or both are over 60.

Enhanced pensioner premium
This applies to single people aged between 75 and 79, and couples where both are under 80, and one or both are between 75 and 79.

Higher pensioner premium
This is given to people aged 80 and over, or aged 60 to 79 and fulfilling the conditions for a disability premium (see below).

Disability premium
This is given to people under 60 getting:

- Attendance Allowance

- Disability Living Allowance

- Severe Disablement Allowance

- long-term rate of Incapacity Benefit, or

- registered as blind.

Severe disability premium
This premium is available in addition to either the disability premium or the higher pensioner premium. It is available to single people living alone, and receiving:

- Attendance Allowance, or

- The middle or highest level of the care component of Disability Living Allowance, provided that nobody is receiving Invalid Care Allowance for looking after them.

Single people not living alone can also claim this premium if they live with:

- someone who also gets Attendance Allowance

- someone who is registered blind

- a paid helper supplied by a charity, or

- if you are a joint tenant, or joint owner and share housing costs.

This premium is also available to couples if one partner receives Attendance Allowance or the middle or highest level of the care component of Disability Living Allowance, provided that:

- the partner also gets Attendance Allowance or the middle or highest rate of the care component of Disability Living Allowance, or is registered blind, *and*

- nobody receives Invalid Care Allowance for looking after the claimant, *and*

- the claimant 'lives alone' as described above.

As you see, these rules are fairly complicated, so it is a good idea to seek help.

Carer premium
This premium is given to carers getting the Invalid Care Allowance. Certain people who applied for Invalid Care Allowance after 1st October 1990 did not receive it because they received another benefit (such as Widows' Pension). Those people can still qualify for the carer premium of Income Support.

Housing Costs
In addition to the premiums, there are additions for certain housing costs. If you are over 60 the help includes mortgage interest, interest on loans for certain repairs or improvements, ground rent, and certain service charges.

These additions may be reduced if other people apart from your partner or dependent child live in your home.

Special circumstances
Certain circumstances affect the Income Support payments. These include living in someone else's home (their Income Support payments may be affected), boarders or hostel dwellers, periods in hospital, and living in residential or nursing homes.

THE SOCIAL FUND

This fund provides lump sum payments, either as loans or as grants, to people on low incomes. Here are some of the 'exceptional cases' which the Social Fund is designed to meet.

Funeral expenses
Funeral expenses of a partner, close relative, or someone else if it is reasonable to expect you to take responsibility. The deceased must have been resident in the UK and the funeral must take place in the UK. Any savings over £500 (or £1,000 if you are over 60) will be taken into account, plus any money from the estate of the deceased person.

Cold weather payments and winter fuel payments
These apply where they are not related to income, as part of the Income Support or State Pension system.

Discretionary Social Fund payments
These may be made on a discretionary basis, and are made either as grants or as loans.

Grants are called 'Community Care Grants', and they are means-tested. They include things such as:

- Help with moving out of residential or institutional care (e.g. a bed, or a cooker).

- Help to enable people to continue living at home (e.g. minor repairs, removals costs to more suitable accommodation).

- Help with exceptional family pressure (e.g. chronic sickness, relationship breakdown).

- Help with certain travel expenses (e.g. attending a relative's funeral, visiting the sick).

Loans are also available. There are two main types:

- Budgeting loans, to help spread the cost of larger one-off expenses.

- Crisis loans, to help cope with emergencies or disasters.

The loans are repayable by deduction from the benefit, normally over 78 weeks, but exceptionally over 104 weeks.

HOUSING BENEFIT AND COUNCIL TAX BENEFIT

These benefits are available to people on low incomes, and with savings of not more than £16,000. For couples, the income and the savings of both partners are counted towards the limits.

Housing Benefit
This is available to help pay rent, either to a council, housing association (also known as Registered Social Landlord) or a private landlord.

It is also available to:

- Boarders and hostel dwellers, for the accommodation part of their charges.

- People living in houseboats, for the mooring charges.

- People living in caravans or mobile homes, for the site charges.

- Joint tenants.

- People living with a landlord who is a close relative – so long as they live in separate, self-contained accommodation.

Council Tax Benefit
The person responsible for paying the Council Tax may be eligible for the Council Tax Benefit. The 'second adult' rebate may also be available if there are one or more people with low incomes living with the main Council Tax payer.

The benefits (Council Tax Benefit and Housing Benefit) are calculated on a similar basis to Income Support, although the figures are not necessarily the same. The process can be summarised as follows:

- Calculate the maximum weekly amount for which you can get benefit.

- Deduct an amount for non-dependants living with you.

- Add up the value of your savings.

- Work out your weekly income.

- Work out the balance available according to the government figures.

The following special circumstances affect the benefit.

Absence from home
If you are in hospital, you can continue receiving the benefits for up to 52 weeks, but there will be a reduction after six weeks. If you are away from home for any other reason, the benefit may be paid dependent on the reason for the absence. If you sub-let your home while you are away, you cannot continue to receive the benefits.

Benefits for two homes
Normally, housing benefit is only payable for one home. However, if you moved and could not avoid liability to pay rent for both homes,

you may get benefit for two homes for up to four weeks. There is no Council Tax Benefit for a second home.

Hardship relief
The local authority may increase the benefit in cases of hardship or exceptional circumstances.

Exemptions
Certain properties can gain exemption from Council Tax. If your former home is empty because you are living in hospital or a residential or nursing home, you can get exemption. You can also get it if you have gone to live with someone to receive or give personal care. A property can also get exemption if a severely mentally impaired person is living there alone.

Disability Reduction scheme
If your home has certain features for disabled people, such as extra space for a wheelchair, or special bathroom facilities, it can benefit by being lowered by one band for the tax assessment. If the home is already in the lowest band (band A), it can benefit from a further reduction.

OTHER BENEFITS

Other state benefits are available, not specifically for older or retired people, but in circumstances which often affect older people. These include a whole range of benefits for people with disabilities (either physical or mental) and their carers.

The main benefits which help with extra costs due to the disability are Attendance Allowance and Disability Living Allowance. Other benefits such as Incapacity Benefit and Severe Disablement Allowance are paid to people unable to work because of their disability. Also, a Disabled Person's Tax Credit is a benefit for people whose disability has limited their earning capacity.

Disablement benefit is paid to compensate for industrial injury, and is paid as an addition to State Retirement Pension or Incapacity Benefit. The level of payment depends on an assessment of the degree of disablement. Constant Attendance Allowance may also be granted if you qualify for the 100% rate. If you permanently need high levels of attention, there is also an Exceptionally Severe Disablement Allowance.

If you are disabled as a result of war or peacetime service in the armed forces, you may get a War Disablement Pension. Again, the amount depends on the degree of disability assessed. The Constant Attendance Allowance may also be granted, together with a Mobility Supplement if the disability causes difficulty in walking.

If your husband's death was due to service in the armed forces, or his death was substantially hastened by that service, you can get a War Widows' Pension.

OTHER HELP

Some benefits or grants are available to help in specific situations.

Home repairs and improvements

Local authorities can give grants for certain work on your house. If you are applying for such a grant, make sure you do not start the work or buy the materials before you get the approval. Some areas have 'Staying Put' schemes to provide help for you to repair or adapt your home to enable you to stay in it rather than going into residential care homes.

Renovation grants
These are for things like installing an inside toilet, or hot and cold water supply. These grants are discretionary and means-tested for income and capital.

Home repair assistance
This covers things like rewiring, insulation and minor adaptations. It is a discretionary grant, and the local authorities have much discretion in deciding who gets this help. It is available if you are:

- over 60, or
- disabled or infirm, or
- receiving a means-tested benefit.

Disabled facilities grants
Available to make life easier for disabled people. If your home needs adaptation to help you get in or out of it or use essential facilities such as bathroom, kitchen or toilet, these grants are usually mandatory. Otherwise, they are discretionary. All these grants are means-tested for income and capital.

Insulation and draughtproofing grants
Available from the Home Energy Efficiency Scheme. If you are:

- over 60, and

- receiving Income Support, Housing Benefit, Council Tax Benefit, or Income Based Jobseekers Allowance,

you are eligible for a 'New HEES Plus' grant. This grant is for energy conservation measures, including:

- change to off-peak electric heating

- central heating for the main living areas

- conversion of open solid fires to closed

- replacement to more efficient boilers

- insulation measures.

Owner occupiers and private tenants are given priority, and the maximum grant is £2,000 at the time of writing. In addition to the grant there is a free security assessment, and window or door locks will also be installed under this system.

Help with health costs
You should be aware of what National Health Service treatments or services are free, and which are free after a certain age.

Hearing aids
If you have hearing difficulties, your GP will arrange a visit to a hospital for tests. NHS hearing aids are loaned free, and batteries and replacements are free. Privately bought aids can be expensive, and are not necessarily more effective.

Chiropody
The NHS provides chiropody services if there is a clinical need. Your GP will be able to assess this, and refer you to a service provider. Otherwise, you will have to get a private chiropodist.

Other NHS costs
There are two basic levels of help with NHS costs for services which are normally charged. The higher level is given if you are:

- receiving Income Support, Income Based Jobseekers Allowance, or Disabled Person's Tax Credit (if you are on a low income), or

- granted a Certificate HC2 under the NHS Low Income Scheme (i.e. with savings under £8,000 and on a low income).

The lower level is given if you are granted a Certificate HC3 (based on the same criteria as HC2, but with higher income level).

Prescriptions
You qualify for free prescriptions if you:

- are aged 60 or over, or

- have the higher level of help described above, or

- suffer from a 'specified medical condition'.

If you have a Certificate HC3, you get partial help with prescription charges. You may also be able to save money on prescriptions by buying a 'season ticket' (formally known as a prepayment certificate).

Dental treatment
You qualify for free treatment if you have the higher level of help described above. If you have Certificate HC3, the charges are reduced. This help does not extend to private dental care. Make sure that your dentist is providing you with NHS dental care each time you get treatment.

Eyesight tests and glasses
You qualify for free sight tests if you:

- are aged 60 or over, or

- have the higher level of help described above, or

- are registered blind or partially sighted, or

- need complex lenses, or

- are diagnosed as a diabetic, or

- have glaucoma, or

- are aged over 40, and you are the parent, brother, sister or child of someone diagnosed with glaucoma.

If you need a test at home, you will not have to pay for the visit if you qualify for free testing. If you are on the higher level of help as described above, you also get a voucher towards the cost of spectacles. If you are entitled to the lower level of help, there is partial help towards testing and spectacle costs.

Elastic hosiery, wigs and fabric supports
These are free if you are entitled to the higher level of help. If you are entitled to the lower level of help, there is some support towards costs.

Hospital travel costs
You can get help with necessary travelling costs to a hospital for NHS treatment if you are receiving Income Support or Income Based Jobseekers Allowance, or Disabled Person's Tax Credit. You can also get a lower level of help if you have Certificate HC2 or HC3.

CHECKLIST

- State benefits can be contributory or non-contributory; dependent on age or not; and means tested or not.

- The state pension can be 'topped up' if your contribution record is inadequate.

- You can protect your state pension rights.

- There may be benefits to claim if you retire early.

- Income Support may be available if you are on a low income.

- The Social Fund may make discretionary loans or grants.

- There is a whole range of other benefits and help available.

- If in doubt, ask your local Social Security office.

CASE STUDIES

Norman defers his pension
Norman is approaching retirement age. He gets a pension forecast, but he will be working on an extra couple of years at the special request of his employer, and at a good rate of pay. He therefore decides to defer his pension to get an increased pension when he finally retires.

Dorothy receives Widows' Pension

Dorothy is widowed at the age of 57, in the year 2000. She receives the lump sum, and the Widows' Pension. At age 60 she elects to receive the state retirement pension. Shortly after, she meets someone she would like to marry. Happily, her pension will not be affected if she remarries.

PERSONAL EVALUATION

1. Do you feel that you have any circumstances which might qualify you for a benefit?

2. If so, what action do you intend to take about it?

3. Are you sure about your past National Insurance contributions?

4. Do you feel it is worth getting a pension forecast?

5. If your contributions are not adequate, would you know how to judge whether it is the right thing to pay voluntary contributions to make up your record?

7

Paying Tax

Taxes are the price we pay for a civilised society. We all have to pay our fair share, whether employed, self-employed or retired.

THE SELF-ASSESSMENT SYSTEM

The self-assessment system has been with us for a few years now (see my book *Coping with Self Assessment,* How To Books). Here is a brief summary of self-assessment as it affects retired people.

COMPLETING THE TAX RETURN

If you have not filled in a tax return before, and you have a source of income that is not taxed at source, you must notify the Inland Revenue by 5th October following the end of the tax year in which you received that source of income. (The tax year runs from 6th April to the following 5th April). If you have sent in a tax return before, then you should receive a tax return shortly after 5th April each year. If you do not receive a tax return, and you continue to receive income liable to tax, then you must notify the Inland Revenue by 5th October following the end of the tax year.

Keeping records

The law requires you to keep such records as are needed to allow you to make a complete and correct tax return. Some records of transactions will come from another source. If so, all you need to do is to make sure you keep them safe. However, you may need to make some records yourself. In general, make a record of any income which is *not supported* by a document sent to you with the income. You can keep this record in any format you wish – a diary, a cash book, or simply a note book.

If you receive property income, you should keep a record of the rents received, and expenses. If you have sold any assets, you must keep a record for Capital Gains Tax purposes of the sales proceeds, the original cost and date of acquisition, and any relevant dates and amounts of valuations.

In normal circumstances (i.e. if you send your tax return in on time) you must retain your records for 22 months after the tax year to which they relate. If you send your tax return in late, you must keep the records for two years after the date you sent your tax return in. If you are undergoing an investigation, you should keep your records until the Inland Revenue tells you that you need no longer retain them.

- Warning – if you receive property income, that is treated for these purposes in the same way as business income. You must retain your records for five years after the normal filing date.

Filling in the tax return

Your tax return consists of the 'core' return, plus any additional pages which the Inspector of Taxes thinks you need. Additional pages relate to different sources of income, such as employment income, self-employment income, partnership income, income from abroad, capital gains, etc.

First, make sure you have all the pages you need. If you have a source of income, but you do not have the correct pages, ask the local tax office for them.

Next, collect together all the information concerning the income from all your sources, and all the claims for allowances and reliefs. Then go through the return and additional pages, filling in all the details of your income and claims. There is a guide booklet which comes with the tax return, and gives you advice about how to fill in the boxes.

When you have filled in the boxes, decide whether you want to calculate the tax yourself or get the Inland Revenue to calculate it. You may ask the Inland Revenue to calculate the tax *only* if you send the return back by 30th September following the end of the tax year. If you send it in after that date, or if you choose to calculate your own tax, there is a tax calculation guide. Work your way through this, and enter the tax payable in the appropriate box in the tax return.

Finally, sign the tax return where indicated. This confirms that you certify that the tax return is correct and complete. Then send it off to the Inland Revenue. It must reach them by 31st January following the tax year at the latest, unless the Inland Revenue sent you the tax return after 31st October following the tax year. In that case, you have three months from the date of issue to send it back.

PAYING THE TAX BILL

The onus is on you to calculate your own tax and pay it when it becomes due. In practice, however, the Inland Revenue sends you a statement of account shortly before your payments become due. The tax is payable as follows:

• The first instalment of tax on account is payable on 31st January in the tax year. This is based on the tax paid in the previous year.

• The second instalment of tax on account is payable the following 31st July.

• The balance of tax for the previous year is payable by 31st January following the end of the tax year.

Payments on account

The payments on account for one year are calculated by reference to the actual tax paid for the previous year. If you think your tax bill should be reduced for the next year, you may apply to reduce the payments on account. However, if you pay too little on account you will have to pay interest on any short payment, from the due date.

If the payments on account are more than the final tax liability for the year, the Inland Revenue will refund the overpayment to you, or deduct it from the next payment due.

Avoiding penalties, interest and surcharges

The Inland Revenue has the power to impose the following penalties, although they can mitigate the penalties if they see good reason.

• Late delivery of tax return:
  – penalty £100 if it is up to six months late
  – penalty £200 more than six months late up to one year late
  – penalty up to 100% of tax due over one year late.

• Delay after the Commissioners direct that you must send in a tax return:
  – £60 per day.

- Failure to keep and retain proper records:
  – up to £3,000 for each failure.

- Failure to produce records requested by Inspector of Taxes in the course of an enquiry:
  – £50, plus £30 per day.

Interest is charged on all late payments on a daily basis at the official rate, which is published by the Inland Revenue from time to time. They emphasise that this is in no way a penalty, but is merely designed to provide commercial restitution for the use of the money. If the Inland Revenue is late in repaying you, they will also pay you interest at the same official rate.

Surcharges are added to tax payable if you pay late. If tax is paid more than 28 days late, up to six months late, the surcharge is 5% of the tax due. If tax is paid more than six months late, the surcharge is 10% of the tax due.

Adjustments and enquiries

Correcting mistakes

If you discover that you have made an error in your tax return, you may amend the tax return by writing to the Inspector of Taxes at any time up to one year from the normal filing date. The Inspector of Taxes may correct any 'manifest mistake' in your tax return within nine months of receiving your tax return, and he must notify you of the corrections.

Enquiries by the Inspector of Taxes

As part of the verification procedure, the Inland Revenue picks out a small number of tax returns at random. These are then subject to enquiry by the Inspector of Taxes. They may also enquire into any tax return if there is an aspect of the figures which they believe requires further investigation.

The Inspector of Taxes does not have to justify an enquiry into your tax return, and you must be ready to provide any information and explanation required.

PAYING LESS TAX

Although we all have to pay our fair share of tax, nobody actually enjoys paying it. You can take steps to ensure that you do not pay more than you should. (See my book *Paying Less Tax*, How To Books.) Here are a few guidelines to help you save tax.

INCOME TAX

Using your allowances
Everybody has a basic tax allowance, and you are only taxed on income that exceeds this figure. Certain other allowances have to be claimed on the tax return. These include blind person's allowance, transitional allowance, married couple's allowance (for those over 65), additional personal allowance, and transfer of surplus allowances between spouses.

Opportunities arise for married couples to make sure they use their personal allowances to the full. If you have control over income, you should try to equalise incomes as far as possible.

Using the tax bands
At the time of writing, there are four tax bands. The first band of income (£1,520 per year) and all dividend income is taxed at 10%. Other investment income (such as interest received) is taxed at 20%. Other income over the lower rate band is taxed at 22%, and all taxable income above £28,400 per year is taxed at 40%.

The lower rates of tax can be considered as a sort of 'allowance'. Once again, if incomes can be equalised between spouses, tax can be minimised.

Sharing the married couple's allowance
The married couple's allowance may be shared between spouses, or allocated to either. This allowance is only given at 10% – not at your highest rate of tax. Therefore, it is only advantageous to vary the allocation where:

- one spouse is not taxable at all, or
- one spouse's tax liability is less than the married couple's allowance (at the 10% rate).

It is also possible to transfer any surplus married couple's allowance not used to the other spouse. You have to sign an election to do this.

Making sure your allowances are not restricted
The tax allowances available when you are over 65 can be restricted

if your income is over a certain limit (at the time of writing this is £17,000 per year). The allowance is restricted by half the amount by which your income exceeds the limit.

If one spouse's income is over the restriction limit, but the other's is not, then you could save tax by transferring some income to the spouse with the lower income.

Using exemptions

Some income is exempt from income tax. The main way of using exemptions is to invest as far as possible in tax exempt investments. Individual Savings Accounts provide the main vehicle.

Timing your transactions

Occasionally it is possible to reduce your tax bill by the timing of your transactions. If you can move income from one year when you suffer a high rate of tax, to another year when you suffer a lower rate of tax, then you pay less tax. This is sometimes possible when you retire. Often, your income reduces so much that, after retirement, you pay a lower rate of tax.

Getting the right kind of tax credit

Sometimes you pay tax by deduction at source, but your final tax liability is less than the tax deducted. You can make a claim to have the excess tax repaid to you. However, if the tax was deducted from dividends, they are not repayable. By contrast, if you receive interest from a bank, or on government stocks, or other companies' loan stocks, the tax deducted *is* repayable.

Therefore you could benefit by having a different type of investment. It would mean selling some shares, and reinvesting in a different type of investment. You must be sure that this would not involve you in any extra tax (such as Capital Gains Tax), and also that the new investment is right for you.

CAPITAL GAINS TAX

As with income tax, everybody has a personal allowance for Capital Gains Tax purposes. This tax is charged by adding the chargeable amount to your investment income for income tax purposes, and calculating what the additional tax would be. Therefore you could benefit by using your personal allowance and your lower rate bands in the same way as for income tax.

Using losses

Capital gains or losses are achieved by selling assets, so you have some degree of control over your liability to this tax. All your transactions in a tax year are put together for Capital Gains Tax purposes, and the net result is liable to tax. There may be some assets which would produce a loss, and you could use those losses to bring your total net gains below the personal allowance limit. This happens most often with stocks and shares.

Timing

If you are approaching the end of the tax year, and you have established gains which would make you taxable, you may be able to realise losses to keep you under the limit. You may also be contemplating the sale of an asset which would take you over the limit for the tax year. If you postponed that transaction until the new tax year, you would avoid any liability in the current year.

There was a practice in years gone by of 'bed and breakfasting' shares. This involved selling shares one day to establish a loss for Capital Gains Tax purposes, then buying those shares back the next day. That is now no longer possible. Any transactions within 30 days of each other are matched for Capital Gains Tax purposes. However, you could still sell shares to establish a loss, then buy other shares. You could also sell the shares, and your spouse could buy them on the same or the next day.

CHECKLIST

- Notify the tax office if you are liable to complete a return.

- Keep adequate records.

- Complete and submit the tax return in time.

- Pay your tax on time.

- Use your allowances and the tax bands to reduce your tax.

- Share the married couple's allowance, and try to keep under the restriction limit for age allowance.

- Use exemptions and timing to keep your tax bill down.

- Get the right kind of tax credits.

- Use losses if available.

CASE STUDIES

Tony relies upon his wife to organise and keep records

Tony has recently retired, and come into an inheritance. He has income from various sources, and he admits he is not very good at organising his paperwork, or accounting for things. His wife has always been the one to organise him. She now takes over responsibility for all the paperwork, and keeps proper files and folders for all their joint income, from several sources – pensions, investments, and income from property.

When the tax return comes she is able to sort out all the information needed and deal with the tax returns for both of them. Tony, however, has to read and sign his own tax return, even though he has largely relied on his wife.

Philip and his wife equalise their incomes

Philip has a fairly substantial company pension, and his wife has the basic state pension. Otherwise, all the investments are in Philip's name. To reduce their tax Philip transfers most of the investments into his wife's name, and utilises both their ISA allowances. This maximises the use of the wife's allowances and lower rate tax bands. Their combined tax bill is considerably reduced.

PERSONAL EVALUATION

1. If you are married, which of you is better organised? Can you agree on who is to do all the administrative work?

2. Do you need to make a record in a diary of any transactions for which you do not have independent verification?

3. Have you arranged your finances so that you have enough money to pay your tax when it is due?

4. Do you feel that your affairs are complex enough to need professional help?

5. Are there ways in which you and your spouse can equalise your incomes?

6. Are there any forms of tax exempt savings of which you could take advantage?

8

Housing in Retirement

SPECIAL NEEDS FOR RETIREMENT HOUSING

When you retire, your housing needs may change. It is not usually a good idea to have many changes to your life in a short period, so you should not necessarily change your house when you retire. But often, as time progresses, your lifestyle changes. Perhaps you find the garden too big to manage and you want a house with a smaller one.

Perhaps you want to be nearer your children. Beware! Children are more likely to move around more frequently these days, so unless you are prepared to move around with them, you may find yourself 'stranded'. Besides, your children may not necessarily want you with them! So before you move away from a place where you have built up friendships, local contacts and so on, think carefully.

Eventually, the time may come when you have to think about whether you need to go into a care home. This often happens when you have become widowed, and coping with the normal household duties is more of a problem. Many people, however, feel that they would like to stay in their own home as long as they can. There are some schemes to help you stay in your own house as long as you can. Sometimes this is achieved by enabling adaptations or improvements to be made to the house. Sometimes all that is needed is a little help with some tasks, because of a disability of some sort.

Help the Aged, a registered charity, has a scheme whereby, if you leave your home to them, they will carry out all sorts of improvements, adaptations and repairs, and guarantee that you can stay there as long as you wish.

SPECIAL RETIREMENT HOUSING DEVELOPMENTS

Many retired people change their housing to the special retirement developments, such as those provided by English Courtyard, a leading company in this field. This can often release capital from the value locked up in your present house.

If you have a large home, and the children have all flown the nest, and you do not need any special nursing or other care, this may be right for you. Retirement housing of this sort is part of a development, with neighbours in the same age bracket as you. Communal chores such as security, gardening, and maintenance are done by paid staff, and there is therefore a regular service charge. It is available to rent or to buy. The properties can be flats or houses, of any size.

Look out for these factors, when choosing:

- Location – is it convenient for your family, and for the things you want to do?

- Services – does it provide the level of services and care you need?

- Surroundings – are the gardens and grounds up to your expectations?

- Neighbours – visit the intended housing and talk to the neighbours.

- Adaptability – can you adapt it to your changing needs?

- Communal areas – are there restrictions on things like car parking for you or your visitors?

- Charges – what are the running costs and service charges?

- Resale value – will the property retain its value?

- Tenure – is it leasehold? If so, how long is the term? Get your solicitor to check out all the terms of the lease.

PAYING FOR CARE

The Social Services department of your local authority manages the assessment of care needs, and the offers of monetary help.

Care at home

Local authorities can arrange care for you in your own home, or some authorities can provide cash payments for you to obtain this care. If they provide cash, you must be able to manage it, and you must not use it to employ a close relative or your spouse to care for you. The local authority will monitor that you are actually spending the money on the care you need.

If you:

- are receiving the highest care component of Disability Living Allowance, and

- have no more than £8,000 savings, and

- receive Income Support or Income Based Jobseekers Allowance

then you may apply for a discretionary grant from the Independent Living Fund, to pay for personal care or household tasks, to enable you to continue living at home.

If the local authority provides care, it has the discretion to charge you for it. Any charge must be reasonable, and you can ask the authority to reduce the charge or waive it altogether. If any services, such as visits by the district nurse, are arranged by the National Health Service, they are free.

Short breaks
The local authority can arrange short breaks (i.e. up to eight weeks) in a residential or nursing home, for which you will be charged. However, if the National Health Service arranges it, it will be free. Other benefits may be affected, depending on how long the break lasts.

Residential or nursing home care
The local authority may arrange for you to go into a private or voluntary home, or into a home run by the authority.

If you go into a private or voluntary home, the local authority will be responsible for payment, but you will have to pay all or part of the charges, according to your financial assessment. If you choose a different home, and it is more expensive, you must have a friend, relative or charity willing to make up the difference.

If you go into a local authority home, you will also be assessed for your financial contribution.

Means-testing
If you have over £16,000 savings you must meet the full fees until your savings fall to £16,000 or less. If your savings are £16,000 or less, you may apply for financial support from the local authority and/or Income Support. The rules for assessing your income and savings are broadly the same as for Income Support (see Chapter 6). The assessment will require a contribution from you to the fees, so as to leave you with a certain net income. At the time of writing this

net income figure with which you are left is £15.45 per week.

The value of your home is taken into account for the 'savings' element of the means-test, unless:

- your stay is only temporary, or
- your partner lives in the home, or
- a relative who is either disabled or over 60 lives there.

The local authority *may* also disregard the value of your home if someone else lives there, such as a friend aged over 60, or a friend or relative under 60 who has been caring for you for a substantial period.

The local authority can place a legal charge on the property, so that the sale of the property is not forced, but when the property is later sold they can recover the money owed from the proceeds of sale. The local authority can also take account of assets which you have transferred to someone else within six months of the authority arranging the residential care.

If you are married your spouse is counted as a 'liable relative'. This means that they can be assessed to contribute to the care costs. There is no nationally agreed figure, so each authority works out its own rules. Thus these arrangements are, strictly speaking, voluntary. However, if the authority does not reach a voluntary agreement, it can apply to the magistrate's court which then has the power to make a binding decision on how much the spouse should pay. However, if you have an unmarried partner they have no liability to contribute.

REALISING THE VALUE IN YOUR HOME

You may have a large value locked up in your home, but how can you use it for your benefit? You could sell the house and use the capital to invest and generate income. However, this has the drawback that you need to find somewhere to live when you have sold your house. You could rent a home, which of course means that you have to be able to rent it for less than the income your investment generates, otherwise you would be out of pocket over the deal.

You could also sell the house, buy a cheaper one, and invest the cash left over. This option could sometimes work if your children have all left home and you do not need such a big house. However, do not underestimate the costs of buying and selling, removing, and doing any necessary improvements to the new house.

Benefiting from home income plans

A number of companies specialise in providing an additional income from the value otherwise locked up in your home. These schemes are aimed at people in their retirement years. In the past some companies offered schemes which were linked to investment bonds, and many people lost money on these type of schemes. They were not really appropriate to the market they were sold to, because they involved a higher degree of risk than was appropriate for the purpose.

The present Home Income Plan market is made up of four main types of plan:

- shared appreciation mortgages
- roll-up loans
- home reversion schemes
- home income plans.

Shared appreciation mortgages

Under this scheme you take out a mortgage secured on your property. You get a lump sum, and you can do what you like with it. The idea is that you invest this to produce an income. You do not have to pay back any interest or capital, as long as you continue to own and live in the house. When you sell your house, or die, the mortgage loan is repaid, and in addition, a percentage (typically 75%) of any increase in the value of the house since you took the loan is also repaid.

This type of scheme cannot be transferred from one house to another, so the loan must be repaid if you move house. This means that if you want to continue the scheme, a fresh loan application must be made each time you move house, incurring extra costs each time. There is no age limit to this scheme.

Roll-up loans

Under this scheme you take out a mortgage secured on your property. You get a lump sum, and you can do with it what you like – again, the idea of this is that you invest it to produce an income. You do not have to make any interest or capital repayments, but the interest is 'rolled up' each year and added to the amount of your loan. The full amount is then repaid when you sell your house or when you die. In times of increasing house values, the increase in the value can keep pace with the increase in the amount of the loan.

Because of the compounding effect of rolling up the interest, you must be very cautious with this type of plan. The interest rates are variable for this type of plan, so that if interest rates increase, the compounding effect gathers pace. This also means that the loan to valuation for this type of plan should be very low – probably no higher than 20% should be considered as safe. A further effect of this is that the longer the plan is likely to be in effect, the greater the risk of running up a large debt. Therefore you should not consider this type of plan until at least age 70.

If the loan reaches a point where there is a danger of the loan catching up with the property value, you may be asked to start making repayments. It could force you into the position of having to sell the house to repay the loan.

Home reversion schemes
Under these schemes you effectively sell your home, in whole or in part, to the reversion company. You then get either a lump sum or an annuity. You are guaranteed the security of living in the home for the rest of your life, either rent free or for only a nominal sum. Then when you sell your house or die, the reversion company gets the proportion of the sale proceeds. This proportion depends on the proportion you sold the company when you took out the scheme.

The amount of lump sum you would get is never the full market value of the house, because the reversion company has to make provision for you living there for the rest of your life. Therefore the older you are, the nearer will be the price you get to the market price.

Home income plans
Under this type of scheme you take out a mortgage up to the maximum for which tax allowance is granted. The proceeds buys an annuity for the rest of your life. This gives you a monthly income, from which the interest on the mortgage is paid, and the balance is then paid to you.

You do not have to make any repayments of capital, and when you die or sell the property the mortgage is repaid. However, because the annuity is unaffected, even if you sold the house and repaid the mortgage, the annuity payments would continue to be paid to you, and now they would be paid without the deduction of the mortgage interest.

Pausing to think

Whatever type of plan you are considering, you must stop to consider various things which could become problems. Things to take into account are:

- Are any valuation, survey fees etc reimbursed by the reversion company?

- Is the scheme transferable if you move house?

- Repairs and insurance – who is responsible?

- Will it affect any Social Security Benefits you receive?

- What do your family think about it?

- What would happen if you took out the scheme as a single person, then married?

- What would happen if you took the scheme out as a married couple, and one of you died?

- What would happen if a family member or friend moved in to care for you or provide companionship?

- What is the minimum age?

- What is the maximum loan to valuation?

- What is the minimum property value?

- Is there any restriction on the type of property (eg house, flat, maisonette)?

CHECKLIST

- Your housing needs may well change when you retire.

- Think carefully about any big decision.

- Special commercial housing developments are available.

- You may be able to get state help with certain repairs or improvements.

- You may be able to get help to stay in your own home as long as possible.

- You may be able to get help for short stays in residential care.

- If you need permanent residential care, work out the means-testing carefully.

- Releasing the value in your home can be done through:
  - shared appreciation mortgages
  - roll-up loans
  - home reversion schemes
  - home income plans.

Try to anticipate problems!

CASE STUDIES

Margaret chooses a commercial retirement development

Margaret has recently been widowed. She wants to continue to live near her children, but finds the family house and garden rather large to manage. She is otherwise in good health, and leads a varied lifestyle, with many interests. She chooses a retirement development nearby, but only after checking the place, paying several visits, and meeting the new neighbours. The flat she has is in a large, elegant building and is very spacious. There is ample room for car parking for her and her visitors. The large gardens are beautifully landscaped, and cared for by the full-time gardener and handyman, who also carries out any repairs or maintenance. Her solicitor has checked the terms of the lease, and the past record of the maintenance charges.

After selling the family house she has spare cash after paying for the new flat, which she invests to bring in more income. This extra income is more than adequate to meet the maintenance charges, so gives her extra income to enjoy a few more of her interests.

Henry and Minnie stay at home

Henry and Minnie are starting to feel their age, and have more difficulty getting around and coping with normal everyday activities. Minnie now has to use a wheelchair for most things.

They get help with adapting their house to provide better wheelchair access, and adaptations to the toilet and bathroom. This enables them to stay put for several more years.

Charles chooses a home income plan

Charles starts to take stock of the lifestyle he wants, and realises that he will need rather more income. He has no dependants, so he has no qualms about a home income plan. (This would mean that he might have less to leave in his estate.) He studies the plans and decides on a shared appreciation mortgage, as he has no plans to move house now. This provides a lump sum which he invests.

PERSONAL EVALUATION

1. Have you planned ahead for your retirement housing needs? If so, how far ahead can you look?

2. Do you feel that a commercial retirement scheme would suit your circumstances?

3. Have you investigated all the government help you can get – to stay at home, or to get any care you need, either at your own home or in residential care?

4. If you are married, how would you approach the prospect of residential care for either or both of you?

5. Do you feel that you are able to consider any of the home income plan type schemes?

6. Are there any other people besides you who you think might be affected by a home income plan?

9

Using the Internet

GETTING STARTED

More and more people are using the Internet. When you are retired you often find more time to do things you have always wanted to do, or new things. The Internet is a good way of starting something new, and of doing familiar things in a new way (see Further Reading).

All you need to get started is a computer equipped with a modem, and a telephone line; or an Internet-enabled mobile phone. Internet access will soon be available through your television set. You will have to make your own choice of Internet provider. More providers are now providing a 'free' service. Some financial companies – banks, for example – also provide a free Internet service if you use their financial services.

Finding your way round

You will quickly realise that the world wide web is used by companies as a gigantic advertising hoarding. Their web sites may have all manner of interesting information, pictures, even games, but their main purpose is to get your business. The web actually does more than simply provide an advertising hoarding – it allows you to interact with the companies whose web sites you visit. This means you can sign up for their products, and even pay for the goods or services online.

Once you realise this aspect, you need not be overawed by it. The sheer volume of information allows you to make informed choices. If you are making a big decision or spending a lot of money, it may well pay you to spend some time researching what is available.

Finding the addresses

The convention for web site addresses is to use lower case letters, and no spaces. The full address might read something like *http://www.moneyweb.co.uk*. it is usual to omit the *http://* part of the address, so that it begins with 'www.' In fact, if you type in the address starting with *www.*, in the address bar on your screen, the *http://* part will be filled in for you.

In some cases, however, the pages are not part of the world wide web, and do not have a *www.* address. In this case the full address is given, including the *http://* part. For instance, the address of Riley's insurance is *http://freespace.virgin.net/rileysinsurance*.

Using search engines

If you are looking for information on the Internet, you may not know the address of the web site you are looking for. In fact, you may not even know what web site you need to go to. Search engines can help you to find the right place on the web. Your Internet service provider will give you access to a selection of search engines. Some of the biggest search engines are:

- Yahoo!
- AltaVista
- HotBot
- Excite
- Lycos
- Mirago.

To find an address in a search engine, simply type in the word or words you are looking for, and the search engine will find all the web sites on its register which refer to that word or subject. However, the world wide web is so vast that the search could come back with hundreds of thousands of results. While this may sound impressive, it would clearly be far too many for you to look at.

You can refine your search – for example, by asking for web sites in the UK only, or by asking for sites in a certain subject group. You can also refine the search by using more than one word, and asking the search engine to look for a group of words as a phrase. For instance you could search for information on insurance. This would throw up many thousands of web sites. If, however, you refined your search to look for 'critical illness insurance' as a phrase, you would then narrow down the search, and get the web sites that are more relevant to you.

You can also refine the search by getting the search engine to exclude certain sites. Thus, if you are looking for information about spices for cookery purposes, you could enter the word 'spice'. This might then produce a large number of hits, but most of them about the Spice Girls. To refine the search, if you ask the search engine for 'spice not girls', it would exclude all web sites with references to the Spice Girls.

Printing out

Printing out the page you have been viewing just takes the press of a button. However, you will find that some web sites have dark backgrounds, with the text in white or a different colour. There may also be a lot of pictures. When you come to print out you can use a lot of ink – and ink cartridges are quite an expensive consumable item! If you do not want to print out the pictures you can set your computer to download text only – you will also find that they load much more quickly.

Disciplining yourself

When you log on to the net you can be tempted to wander wherever the fancy takes you. When you are looking something up all sorts of other interesting sites are suggested, either by links from the site you are looking at, or by a search engine.

When you go on to the Internet for a session, decide just what you want from that session. If you are looking for something specific, go straight to it, and do not let yourself be diverted. If you are finding out more about a subject, you may want to wander. At all events, set yourself a time limit.

Communicating

The Internet is not just the world wide web. It is a way of communicating with others. Your Internet service provider will have some channels to 'chat rooms'. These are spaces where you can talk to other people about your favourite subject, or a subject of the moment. These chat rooms have different topics, and practically all the channels have chat rooms devoted to money matters.

Many sites have bulletin boards, where you can post messages, which will provoke responses from other users.

You can think of these bulletin boards or chat rooms as 'cyber clubs' where you can exchange tips or the latest information. But you must use common sense. The site operators always disclaim any responsibility for information posted on bulletin boards or chat rooms. Some people have tried to use these resources to post misleading information, and thereby manipulate prices of shares. Learn to judge the quality of the information.

Getting the best deals and keeping up to date

If you have time, you can often save yourself much effort by looking round the Internet for the best deals. Whatever you are looking for, from investments for your money to insurance for your house, or furniture, you are bound to find it on the Internet. Even if you are not happy about buying over the Internet, you can still use it to compare prices and terms.

In the world of money, things are changing all the time. You can use the Internet to make sure you keep up to date with the very latest products and services on offer.

Have fun!

The Internet is dynamic, interesting and fun. It is a relatively new technology, and is constantly changing. There is a steep learning curve involved – but once you are up and running you will find your own way around the Internet. You will find it is an unrivalled source of information.

SECURITY AND REGULATION ON THE INTERNET

The Internet can be a great place to get all sorts of information about investments – and about money matters in general. Always bear in mind however that the companies with web sites use them as marketing tools. They want you to buy their products. Also, of course, the Internet is an ideal place for all sorts of frauds and scams.

Remember the golden rule – if something looks too good to be true, it probably is. However, when buying goods or services of any sort over the Internet, you cannot physically see or handle what you are buying. Always make absolutely sure exactly what it is that you are buying. If you do not understand a description, ask for more information. Any reputable company will give you all the information about their products or services. This includes such things as:

- delivery dates
- returns of goods
- 'cooling off' periods during which you have the right to change your mind
- guarantees.

Not long ago, www.new-utopia.com attracted many people to invest over the Internet. It promised citizenship of a new 'principality' to be built on a chain of coral reefs in the Caribbean. The US Securities and Exchange Commission shut it down, and froze all the assets, after judging it to be fraudulent.

The SEC in the USA, and the British Financial Services Authority, regulate investment business. They are always on the lookout for frauds perpetrated through the Internet.

There are also independent and government sites which look out for fraud and scams.

REGULATORY AND GOVERNMENT BODIES

The Bank of England
www.bankofengland.co.uk
This is the ultimate regulator of all banking activity in the UK. Its web site is informative, but you would probably need to know much about economics and finance to understand all of the press releases, publications, etc. However, for the more casual browser there is the section about the museum, with much of interest.

Financial Services Authority
www.fsa.gov.uk
This is the regulatory body for the financial services authority, and it has government backing.

The site tells you all about how the industry is regulated, and how to contact the FSA if you need to. It has a page called 'Investor alerts'. Some recent ones include:

- Warning on telephone scam. Be on your guard against telephone callers who pose as bank or building society officials and ask for your account details, in an attempt to get at your money.

- Have you lost out on your pension? Information about the pensions mis-selling scandal.

- Warning on 'copycat' sites. Make sure you don't get taken in by bogus web sites.

- Investing over the Internet: a one-minute exercise. This page takes 60 seconds to read, but could save you a fortune.

This is a well designed site, and user friendly.

The Insurance Ombudsman Bureau
www.thejob.org.uk
This is the site of an organisation set up by the insurance industry to resolve disputes between the public and insurance companies. It should, of course, only be used if you cannot first resolve the dispute with the company itself.

You can send a complaint by email, and they will tell you the correct procedure to follow.

The London Stock Exchange
www.londonstockex.co.uk
This is the official site of the London Stock Exchange. It will tell you almost anything you want to know about the Exchange and its members.

Office of Fair Trading
www.oft.gov.uk
The OFT is a British Government department. The web site gives links to various other organisations around the world working for fair trade and consumer protection. You can operate a wordsearch on this site, to find references to your subject in speeches, official leaflets, etc.

The OFT site has information to help you understand financial products such as mortgages.

Occupational Pensions Regulatory Authority
www.opra.gov.uk
This body regulates company pension schemes, making sure they are properly run, and the funds properly invested. There is a pension tracing service, which may help you to track down a company pension you have lost.

MEMBERSHIP BODIES

These are bodies which have a membership, and can exercise some kind of discipline and regulatory oversight of the members.

The Annuity Bureau
www. annuity-bureau.co.uk
This organisation provides information about pensions and annuities.

Association of British Insurers
www.abi.org
This is the body for insurance companies and pension companies. It has a consumer information service.

Association of Unit Trust and Investment Funds (AUTIF)
www.investmentfunds.org.uk

Association of Investment Trust Companies (AITC)
www.aitc.co.uk

Institute of Financial Planning
www.financialplanning.org.uk

Independent Financial Advisers Association (IFAA)
www.ifaa.org.uk

IFA Promotion Ltd
www.unbiased.co.uk
This is actually an organisation that promotes Independent Financial Advisers. They will send you the names and addresses of three local Independent Financial Advisers, and a voucher for a free 'no obligation' consultation.

The National Association of Pension Funds
www.napf.co.uk
This site is designed for pension fund managers, and it can provide information on legislation affecting pensions.

The Pensions Advisory Service
www.opas.org.uk
This site explains the powers of the organisation. It can help in disputes or sorting out problems with pension schemes.

WATCHDOG BODIES

Advertising Standards Authority
www.asa.org.uk
This organisation monitors advertisements, whether on the Internet or not. It offers advice to consumers, and carries weight with commercial advertisers. Its aim is to ensure that advertisements are

legal, decent, honest and truthful. It is an independent body, and although not a government organisation it does have certain powers. Its scope covers advertisements and promotions in non-broadcast media. This includes things like newspaper and magazine advertisements, hoardings, competitions and prize draws.

The web site gives a summary of all its adjudications, listed each month.

Internet Scam Busters

www.scambusters.com

This is an American site, and it is in the form of an e-zine. You will have to register, but it is free of charge. There is a large range of articles about various types of Internet fraud. Again, it is worth a visit, to put you on your guard. The types of fraud are changing all the time, and subscribers to this e-zine keep it up to date.

Internet Fraud Watch

www.fraud.org

Yet another American site – this time, the web site of the National Consumers League. This is an American consumers' organisation, which is updated by its members on frauds and scams of all kinds.

Moneyweb

www.moneyweb.co.uk

This site has several articles about scams and cons current at the time of writing this. There is also a 'guide for educated cynics' about how to read the performance statistics published by insurance and investment companies – and how not to be misled by them.

The Plain English Campaign

www.plainenglish.co.uk

This site and organisation does not have an explicitly 'watchdog' function, but encourages organisations of all kinds to use plain, simple English. It awards its 'crystal mark' for good examples. It also publishes guides, one of which is a guide to pensions. This can be helpful in cutting through the jargon to understand this subject properly.

Standard and Poors

www.standardandpoors.com

This is the leading company for assessing and rating various financial organisations. Its ratings give an indication of the creditworthiness of companies, and the general reliability of funds such as unit trusts or investment trusts. If a fund or company has a high rating, it is sure to make much of this in its advertising and on its web site. The ratings are universally regarded as one of the best independent sources.

CREDIT CARD AND BANKING SECURITY

One of the concerns about doing business on the Internet is the security of credit card information. On the whole, provided that the company you are dealing with has secured their site, security is at least as good, if not better, than using your credit card over the telephone.

The security of this information comes by means of encryption. This is a way of 'scrambling' any information sent via a certain page of a web site. It can then only be unscrambled by the genuine receiver of the information. This service should be available from any company which expects you to make an order for goods or services over the Internet. It is also, of course, an essential part of Internet banking procedure.

In the final analysis, the security of your credit card details rests with the company you are dealing with. It makes sense then to satisfy yourself that they are who they claim to be. A common ploy of fraudsters is to register a web site with a similar name to one which is well known. Also, registration of a 'domain name' (the web site) can be made in one country, while the actual person or company is in a different country. Make sure you know the actual geographical address of the company you are dealing with.

Encryption is offered on current versions of the browsers from Netscape Navigator and Internet Explorer. A small padlock icon in the bottom left-hand corner of the screen indicates 40-bit encryption, and a large padlock icon indicates 128-bit encryption (a higher level of encryption).

- Remember – if in doubt, don't.

CHECKLIST

1. Use the Internet as a tool – don't let it control you.

2. Discipline yourself.

3. Always be wary of something that sounds too good to be true.

4. If you are buying goods or services, make sure that you know the company you are dealing with, and that you have all the information you need.

5. If you are giving your credit card or bank details, make sure the connection is secure. You can check with regulatory bodies or watchdog bodies if you are unsure.

CASE STUDIES

Henry gets addicted!

Henry is recently retired and has always wondered what the Internet is all about. He buys a home computer, and gets connected to the Internet. At first he is apprehensive about dealing with any business or financial matters on the Internet. However, as he starts to gain confidence he deals with more and more.

As he discovers the potential of the Internet, he spends more time on it, until his wife starts to complain that she is becoming an 'Internet widow'.

George resorts to the Insurance Ombudsman

George has had a bad experience with an insurance company which will not entertain his claim. They say it is excluded under the small print of the policy. George feels he was not fully informed about this. He immediately sends an email to the Insurance Ombudsman – full of venom about the insurance company!

The Insurance Ombudsman sends a reply, telling him how to go about pursuing his complaint – firstly by writing to the company, and only then resorting to the Insurance Ombudsman if the complaint is not resolved satisfactorily.

Terry discovers a bogus web site

Terry has found a web site that appeared to be from an independent financial adviser. However, he is vaguely uneasy about some of the claims made on the site. He emails the IFAA and the Financial Services Authority, to enquire about the site. They confirm that the site is, indeed, bogus. The IFAA directs him to the site of IFA Promotion Ltd who can recommend genuine independent advisers in his area.

PERSONAL EVALUATION

1. Do you feel that the Internet is just a fad which will have its day then vanish?

2. Can you think of any ways in which the Internet might help you in your retirement?

10

Planning Beyond the Grave

In this world, nothing can be said to be certain except death and taxes.
Benjamin Franklin

PASSING ON YOUR WEALTH

In retirement people often start to think about the great inevitable fact – that your stay here is temporary. That brings in its train many things which are not in the scope of this book. However, there is one money matter which it brings into sharp focus. How do you pass on your wealth to the next generation, without suffering the ravages of inheritance tax?

Inheritance tax is one that does not strike until you have died, so it may seem unnecessary to plan to pay less. However, this tax strikes at your dependants. Therefore, unless you really want the Inland Revenue to inherit some of your estate, at the expense of your survivors, you ought to think about this tax.

Inheritance tax is payable on death, at a rate of 40% on any of your estate that exceeds £234,000. The first £234,000 is at a nil rate.

Lifetime transfers

There is also a lower rate of tax (20%) on some transfers of assets during your lifetime. The transfers which are caught by this tax are transfers into a discretionary trust. Again, however, the first £234,000 is at a nil rate, and only the excess over £234,000 is taxed at 20%.

A discretionary trust is one by which the trustees have discretion to make payments of income out of the trust, and also to decide the shares of the capital of the trust each potential beneficiary will receive.

There is also a periodical tax charge on these trusts every ten years, and an 'exit' tax charge when a distribution of capital is made from the trust.

Inheritance tax on death

The tax is charged on the value of all assets of the deceased, if he or she is domiciled in the UK. If domiciled outside the UK, the tax is only charged on assets situated in the UK. It is also charged on gifts or transfers made during the seven years before death. However, assets passing to the spouse of the deceased are exempt from this tax. If you die leaving a spouse, therefore, anything you leave him or her is free of tax. However, anything else left to anybody else, including other members of your family, is liable to the tax if your estate is over £234,000.

Potentially exempt transfers

Transfers of value can be made without any liability as long as the donor survives seven years after making them. Potentially exempt transfers are any gifts or transfers made to:

- another individual
- an 'Interest in Possession' trust
- an 'Accumulation and Maintenance' trust, or
- a trust for a mentally or physically disabled person.

Any transfers or gifts not falling within these categories are chargeable transfers.

To claim the relief of a potentially exempt transfer, it is important to keep as full records as possible about your financial transactions. Thus, when you die and your executor comes to sort out your estate, they will have records of the dates and persons to whom you have made transfers.

Tapering the relief

If a person has made one or more potentially exempt transfers, and dies within the seven years, the value of the gift or transfer is brought into the estate, but the tax on them is reduced by the following table:

Number of complete years since the gift was made	Percentage of tax payable on death
Not more than 3	100%
More than 3 but less than 4	80%
More than 4 but less than 5	60%
More than 5 but less than 6	40%
More than 6 but less than 7	20%
More than 7	NIL

Exempt transfers

Apart from the potentially exempt transfers, some transfers or gifts are exempt without any qualification. These can therefore be used as a tool to pay less inheritance tax. The exempt transfers are as follows.

Transfers between husband and wife

We have already seen that anything passing between husband and wife at death is exempt. Anything passing between husband and wife during lifetime is also exempt. There are a couple of points to note, however.

1. This exemption only applies to husband and wife. Unmarried people living together do not qualify for this exemption, even if one is wholly dependent on the other.

2. If the recipient of the gift or transfer is not domiciled in the UK, the exemption is limited to £55,000.

Annual exemption

Everybody is allowed to give away £3,000 each tax year free of inheritance tax. Further, if you do not use up this exemption in one tax year, it can be carried forward and used the next year. However, this carry forward is only valid for one year. It cannot be carried forward any more than one year.

Small gifts exemption

Everybody may give away as many outright gifts as they like in a tax year, up to a total of £250 for each receiver of these gifts. Any gift over £250 is not exempt on the whole amount – not just the excess over £250.

Wedding gifts

You may make wedding gifts free of inheritance tax to either the bride or the groom. These gifts are exempt up to certain limits depending on the relationship between the giver and the receiver, as follows:

- A parent   £5,000
- A grandparent or great grandparent   £2,500
- Anyone else   £1,000

The bride and groom can also give each other wedding gifts before the wedding up to £2,500 each. After the wedding, of course, all gifts and transfers are exempt, because they are between husband and wife.

Normal expenditure from income
Any regular gifts made from income are exempt, provided that they do not reduce the usual standard of living, and that they are made out of income, not capital.

To qualify for this exemption it is usually necessary to establish a pattern of gifts, over a period of years. It is also necessary to be able to prove that the gifts were made out of income, not capital.

Family maintenance gifts
Gifts made for the maintenance of a spouse, child or dependent relative are exempt. This definition includes illegitimate children, step-children and adopted children.

Gifts to political parties and charities
Gifts of any amount to registered charities and the main political parties are exempt from tax – whether made during your lifetime, or passing on your death.

Once again, the key to getting relief for exempt transfers is to keep as full a record as possible. This is particularly important if there is the possibility of establishing a regular pattern of gifts for the 'normal expenditure from income' exemption.

PLANNING FOR INHERITANCE TAX

Planning for inheritance tax involves decisions which sometimes extend beyond merely financial considerations. These decisions are often very personal by nature, and frequently involve your family – both close family and more distant relatives. Therefore it is a good idea to discuss these plans at least with your most immediate family.

Also, these decisions, more than any other related to tax saving, are likely to benefit from consultation with professionals – tax advisers or solicitors.

Finally, whatever the government in power, the earlier you make these decisions the better.

Basic considerations

When making any plans to save inheritance tax you must always ensure that you, or your potential widow or widower, has enough income to live on as comfortably as possible. It is no use living in tax efficient poverty! For this reason, planning earlier in your life for an adequate pension is important. It means that there will be less pressure to hold on to assets later in life because they are needed to generate an income.

SHARING ASSETS

As a general rule of thumb, husbands and wives should normally share their assets as equally as they can. This is useful not only for inheritance tax, but also for other taxes. Each spouse can then make full use of the exemptions and the nil rate band.

Question
Is it always beneficial to divide assets equally between husband and wife?

Answer
This is the general rule. Assets are better shared equally. However, there may be circumstances when one spouse does not want to relinquish a hold on part of the assets. This is particularly noticeable if the marriage itself is not stable.

MAKING A WILL

Apart from the administrative difficulties, not leaving a will can cost your survivors. A will should take into account the inheritance tax liability and the way it strikes.

For instance, if all your estate is left to your spouse, that could be a missed opportunity. This is because all transfers between husband and wife are exempt anyway. Therefore you could leave an amount up to the limit of the nil rate band (currently £234,000) to the next generation, or other beneficiaries, without any liability.

Again, it must be emphasised that this must only be done if there is adequate money for the surviving spouse to live on. Also, it is not worth passing down more than the nil rate band, because it would mean paying inheritance tax earlier than necessary.

It may be possible for the surviving beneficiaries to agree on a 'deed of variation' within two years of the death. This can take effect as if the terms were written in the original will. However, a recent court case has created inheritance tax problems for certain variations. It is always best to have a properly drafted will in the first place.

USING LIFE ASSURANCE

This can be particularly useful for married couples. The inheritance tax charge normally comes on the second death. A life assurance policy written in trust for the survivors can play an important role in providing the funds to pay the inheritance tax. If a policy is written in trust, the proceeds on the second death are outside the estate, and therefore do not count towards the estate on which the tax is charged. If it is written on the joint lives, to pay out on the second death, the premium is normally much lower. If a couple start paying the premiums early in their lives the premiums will normally be much lower, and the premiums can become part of their normal expenditure from income and thereby an exempt transfer.

USING TRUSTS

As we have seen, trusts are a technical area which will need the advice and help of a solicitor. Discretionary trusts are the most flexible, since the trustee has absolute discretion to distribute the income and capital. If you give money into a trust you may also be a trustee, so you may retain control over the money given into the trust while it is outside of your estate. However, as we have seen earlier in this chapter, discretionary trusts do suffer tax charges before you die.

There are other types of trust. An accumulation and maintenance trust is normally set up for children or grandchildren. Money given by you into an accumulation and maintenance trust is a potentially exempt transfer. There is therefore no immediate tax charge, and none at all if you survive seven years. Under this type of trust, the income must be accumulated for the child until they reach an age between 18 and 25. However, the trustee may distribute income from the trust for the maintenance and education of the children. In order to qualify for the potentially exempt status, the trust must:

- Have beneficiaries who are all grandchildren of a common grandparent, and are aged under 25 at the time the trust is made.

- Ensure that the beneficiaries become entitled to the income of the trust at age 25 at the latest. The capital may pass at a later date.

- Accumulate any income not applied to the maintenance or education of the beneficiaries.

An 'interest in possession' trust is one by which certain beneficiaries may enjoy the income of the trust for their lifetime; on their death the capital of the trust is paid out according to the wishes of the person who made the trust. If the person who gives the money into this type of trust is also a trustee, he or she may vary the way in which the income of the trust is distributed while he or she is alive.

Whichever type of trust is made, it does have the benefit of being able to protect the assets. If the trust is properly worded it can protect assets from divorce, creditors, or predatory step-relatives. It can even protect the assets from the beneficiary while that beneficiary is young or immature.

MAKING GIFTS

You may take advantage of gifts during your lifetime to reduce the ultimate inheritance tax liability on your estate. The combined effect of the nil rate band and the seven year cumulative rule for potentially exempt transfers can often go a long way to mitigating this tax. Gifts do not, of course, have to be made in money, but they can be any other assets. When deciding what assets to give, think about their future potential. The value of the gift for these purposes is the value of the gift at the time it is given. Therefore, it is more tax efficient to give a gift that is likely to increase in value. This way any increase in value of that asset comes outside your estate.

If, for example, you have a property that is let to an elderly person, that property would increase in value when the tenant dies. (An empty property is always worth more than a tenanted one.)

There are two points to remember, however.

- First, the gift must be given outright. There must be no 'reservation of benefit'. For instance, if you gave your house to your children, but carried on living in it without paying the full market rent, that would be a gift with reservation of benefit. Any such gifts are not potentially exempt transfers. They are still counted as part of your estate when you die.

- Secondly, you should not give away more than you can afford. It is no use to leave your survivors free of inheritance tax if the price is that you live in poverty for the rest of your life. This point has been made already, but it is worth repeating.

USING RELIEFS

There are some very valuable reliefs for business property and agricultural land. The relief can be at 100% or at 50%, depending on the circumstances. There are fairly complex rules, relating to the period of ownership, the type of business structure, whether land is tenanted and so on. (See *Paying Less Tax*, Further Reading for more details.)

CHECKLIST

1. Think about passing on your wealth and the impact of inheritance tax.

2. Try to plan to limit the impact of inheritance tax.

3. Try to share assets as equally as possible.

4. Make a will.

5. Use life assurance or trusts if appropriate.

6. Get professional advice.

CASE STUDIES

Dennis and Maggie revise their wills

Dennis and Maggie are well into retirement, and quite well off. They have a son and a daughter, and several grandchildren. The subject of their inheritance tax plans has been sparked off by the first of their grandchildren to get married. They take advantage straight away of the exemption and give a wedding gift to their grandson of £2,500. They then feel that they could well afford to give away certain other gifts without prejudicing their standard of living. They have not used up their annual exemption this tax year or last year, so they can give away up to £12,000 between them. They give £4,000 each to their two children, and £1,000 each to their remaining four grandchildren.

They then give some attention to their wills. They amend their wills so as to leave £200,000 (almost the extent of the nil rate band) amongst their children and grandchildren. They then leave the rest of their estates to each other. They had already equalised their estates as far as practicable in a previous exercise. The house is held jointly, and their investments are held more or less equally. Even after giving £200,000 away on the first death, the survivor will have an adequate income. There would then be a small amount of inheritance tax to pay, but they reckon that they have done enough now to substantially ease the burden of inheritance tax.

Neil and Glenys pay a life assurance premium

Neil and Glenys are also fairly well off, but not as well off as Dennis and Maggie. Having considered their inheritance tax position, they decide to take out a life assurance policy written in trust for their survivors (they have three children and three grandchildren). The policy is written for the benefit to become payable on the second death. The policy is for the current estimated amount of inheritance tax which would be payable. The premium is comfortably affordable, and comes within their annual exemption.

They do not amend their wills. They have left everything to each other, so that the inheritance tax liability will only apply on the second death.

PERSONAL EVALUATION

1. Do you and your spouse have wills? Are they regularly revised in the light of changing circumstances?

2. Have you passed on as much as you want your children and grandchildren to have before your death?

3. Do you make full use of the exempt transfers?

4. How are your assets divided between you and your spouse? Could they be better divided for inheritance tax purposes?

5. Have you considered the use of trusts or life assurance policies?

Glossary

Capital Gains Tax. A tax on the profit made on disposing of assets.

Collective investment. An investment in a fund which invests in other shares, and spreads the risk.

Government stocks. A loan to the government on which you receive interest.

Home income plans. Schemes to enable you to realise the value locked up in your home.

Income Support. A non-contributory benefit of Social Security.

Index. An indicator of the price movements of a specific group of shares.

Inheritance tax. A tax on the wealth passed on when someone dies.

Internet. Connections between computers enabling them to communicate with each other.

Personal pensions. A government approved scheme to provide a pension for yourself, attracting tax relief.

Portfolio. The sum total of all your investments.

Self-assessment. The method of assessing and collecting tax in this country.

Shares. A unit of ownership of a company.

Social Fund. A fund of Social Security, providing grants or loans for exceptional circumstances.

Social Security. The state system of providing security. Contributions are made into the system when you work, and benefits are drawn out when you retire or cannot work.

Stockbroker. An intermediary between the general public and the market makers on a stock exchange.

Stock exchange. An organisation enabling shares and securities to be traded.

Superannuation. A scheme provided by an employer to provide a pension when you retire.

Will. The legal document by which you dispose of your estate when you die.

Yield. The actual return you would get by buying an investment at the price quoted.

Useful Contacts and Addresses

CHARITIES

There are many charities that can provide help. Some are connected to specific occupations. Some are general charities. Some provide financial help. Others provide help in different ways. Most public libraries have a copy of *Charities Digest*, which gives a summary of the help offered by many charities. The Directory of Social Change also publishes *A Guide to Grants for Individuals in Need*. There are also two organisations to help put you in touch with charities that may be able to help you. These are The Association of Charity Officers, and Charity Search.

Water rates
Some water companies have charitable funds to help people in financial need.

Blindness
The Royal National Institute for the Blind (RNIB) offers advice and information for blind and partially sighted people on many issues, including Social Security matters.

Hearing
The Royal National Institute for the Deaf (RNID) produces information leaflets on hearing aids, hearing loss and other deafness-related matters.

General help
Age Concern
A charity which gives a great deal of information on many subjects. They publish a large number of factsheets. You may receive up to five factsheets free, by telephoning their Information Line (Freephone 0800 00 99 66), or by writing (see below). There is also a factsheet subscription service which gives you all the factsheets in a

folder, with regular updates throughout the year. The first year's subscription is £70 at the time of writing.

Age Concern also has an insurance services company dealing in insurances for:

- home and contents
- car
- motor breakdown
- pets
- travel.

Many local areas also have an Age Concern sponsored 'advocacy' service. This provides free independent help and support (but not legal support). The 'advocate' helps by providing support for those who cannot speak out for themselves, and helping discover the best course of action from various options.

Age Concern, Astral House, 1268 London Road, London, SW16 4ER.

The Citizens' Advice Bureau
A well known organisation which provides on-the-spot advice on all kinds of matters. Even if the person cannot help you, they will be able to tell you where to find help.

Law centres
These exist in many parts of the country, giving free legal advice. The Law Centres Federation will be able to tell you where your nearest centre is.

Association of Unit Trusts and Investment Funds
65 Kingsway, London WC2.

Building Societies Association
3 Saville Row, London W1.

Ethical Investment Research Service
504 Bondway Business Centre, 71 Bondway, London SW8 1SQ.

London Stock Exchange Public Information Department
London Stock Exchange, London EC2N 1HP.

National Savings Sales Information Unit
Freepost BJ2092, Blackpool FY3 9XR.

THE INTERNET – SOME FINANCIAL WEB SITE ADDRESSES

The London Stock Exchange – *www.londonstockex.co.uk*
Updata (provides investments tools) – *www.updata.co.uk*
Inland Revenue – *www.inlandrevenue.gov.uk*
Chartered Accountants – *www. chartered-accountants.co.uk*
Financial Times – *www.ft.com*
Financial Information Net Directory (a link to many other sites) –
   www.find.co.uk
Interactive Investor International – *www.iii.co.uk*
Money Shop (a link to many other sites) – *www.moneyshop.co.uk*
Motley Fool (a famous online money magazine) – *www.fool.co.uk*

Further Reading

Coping with Self Assessment, John Whiteley (How To Books).
Investing in Stock and Shares, Dr John White (How To Books).
Investment Made Easy, Jim Slater (Orion Books).
Managing Your Personal Finances, John Claxton (How To Books).
Paying Less Tax, John Whiteley (How To Books).
Personal Finance on the Net, John Whiteley (How To Books). Looks at the many ways in which you can use the Internet to help you handle your money.
Saving and Investing, John Whiteley (How To Books).
Securing a Rewarding Retirement, Norman Toulson (How To Books).
The Ethical Investor, Russell Sparkes (Harper Collins).
The Online Investor, Peter Temple (John Wiley).
The Zulu Principle, Jim Slater (Orion Books).
Using the Internet, Graham Jones (How To Books). A good starting point if you have never used the Internet.

Index

MANAGING YOUR PERSONAL FINANCES
How to achieve your own financial security, wealth and independence

John Claxton

Start to control your money – instead of letting it control you. This book shows you how to become your own financial advisor. Find out how to protect your income, invest surplus funds, reduce your tax bill and develop your own financial strategy. The methods are here, together with lots of sound ideas to help rid you of money worries once and for all. '...includes tips on [how to] avoid debt, finance your retirement, acquire new financial skills, increase your income and much more.' *The Express.* John Claxton is a successful Chartered Management Accountant and Chartered Secretary who also teaches personal finance.

160pp. illus. 1 85703 581 X. 4th edition

PAYING LESS TAX
How to keep more of your money for saving and investing

John Whiteley

This money-saving book reveals how you can pay less tax – and not just on what you earn. Value added, capital gains, inheritance, and business tax are covered too, with special sections on forming partnerships and limited companies. Discover how to take advantage of allowances, reliefs and exemptions, and avoid interest, penalties and surcharges. Whatever your age or status, this book will have something for you. From timing your transactions so as to reap maximum benefit, to the pros and cons of tax exile. 'Extremely practical and digestible.' *Financial Mail on Sunday.*

144pp. illus. 1 85703 579 8. 2nd edition

PERSONAL FINANCE ON THE NET
Use the power of the Internet to grow your personal wealth

John Whiteley

Find the best rates for your savings, get great mortgage deals, and deal with your taxes – all via the Internet. You can bank online too, take up life assurance and plan your pension. And this enlightening book gives you true professional advice in addition to lists of useful web sites. Discover more about investments and stock brokers, know what to insure against, use tax incentives and a whole host of other things to help you get the most from your money.

144pp. illus. 1 85703 594 1

COPING WITH SELF ASSESSMENT
How to complete your tax return and minimise your tax bill

John Whiteley

'If you dare to do your own tax return, this book needs to be on your bookshelf.' Laurel Alexander, *Working From Home*. Save time and money with this step-by-step-guide. It takes you through everything from completing the forms correctly to surviving an Inland Revenue enquiry. What do you do if you make an error in your claim and how do you make payments on account? The answers are all here, together with ways to avoid penalties, interest and surcharges, plus a chapter on paying less tax. John Whiteley is a Chartered Accountant who has successfully advised taxpayers from all walks of life.

160pp. illus. 1 85703 580 1. 4th edition

INVESTING IN STOCKS & SHARES
A step-by-step guide to increasing your wealth as a personal investor

Dr John White

Updated with the most recent developments in the stock market, this reliable guide shows you the best way to invest in stocks and shares for yourself. It looks at share prices, avoiding undue risks and how to deal on the stock market. Futures, traded options, bonds and gilts are all explored too, and you're given step-by-step guidance throughout. 'If you have got money to spare, start by investing in the purchase of this book.' *Making Money.* 'Will be a help to private investors...an easy to understand guide.' *What Investment.* Dr John White is a successful investor, and director of an investment company. He has also written a range of chart-analysis software for stock market investment.

224pp. illus. 1 85703 582 8. 5th edition

MAKING YOUR MONEY WORK FOR YOU
How to use simple investment principles to increase your wealth

Simon Collins

This book takes a fresh approach to investment, putting you in the driving seat. In simple, jargon-free language, City investor Simon Collins explains the principles that underlie all investment decisions, both financial and non-financial. These are straightforward techniques for managing your own money, whether your interest is in shares, gold, or even antique china.]

128pp. illus. 1 85703 462 7

USING THE INTERNET
How to get started and find what you want for business, education and pleasure

Graham Jones

'A comprehensive guide for the novice...The book is well-versed in the latest technology...a useful guide.' *Computeractive.* 'Practical, down-to-earth advice.' *Focus on Business Education.* 'A good introduction to Internet basics.' *Working From Home.*

128pp. illus. 1 85703 504 6. 3rd edition

SAVING & INVESTING
How to achieve financial security and make your money grow

John Whiteley

You don't have to be rich to start saving and investing. This straightforward guide, now in its third updated edition, is written for ordinary people who want to take control of their financial destiny. John Whiteley draws on his substantial experience as a Chartered Accountant to set out simple guidelines which enable readers to find their own best route to financial security. Find out how to decide and set financial goals, manage savings and investments, benefit from tax incentives and release the value in your home and monitor results.

128pp. illus. 1 85703 583 6. 3rd edition